HISTORIC TALES OF
GASPARILLA ISLAND

HISTORIC TALES OF
GASPARILLA ISLAND

DAVID FUTCH

THE
History
PRESS

Published by The History Press
Charleston, SC
www.historypress.com

Cover image: The oil-on-plywood *Pilikia* hung behind the Pink Elephant Bar for decades as a reminder of why people made way to Gasparilla Island— fishing and fun. In a subscript, one of the men says to his buddy, "What the hell are we drinking, anyway?" Photo of Betsy Fugate Joiner's *Pilikia* by Rick Montgomery of Island TV.
Back cover: courtesy Wickman's Photo Shop; *top insert*: courtesy Betsy Fugate Joiner; *middle insert*: courtesy of the Futch family; *bottom insert*: courtesy of All Engelhard and Sophie Engelhard Craighead.

First published 2022

Manufactured in the United States

ISBN 9781467151702

Library of Congress Control Number: 2021950617

Notice: The information in this book is true and complete to the best of our knowledge. It is offered without guarantee on the part of the author or The History Press. The author and The History Press disclaim all liability in connection with the use of this book.

CONTENTS

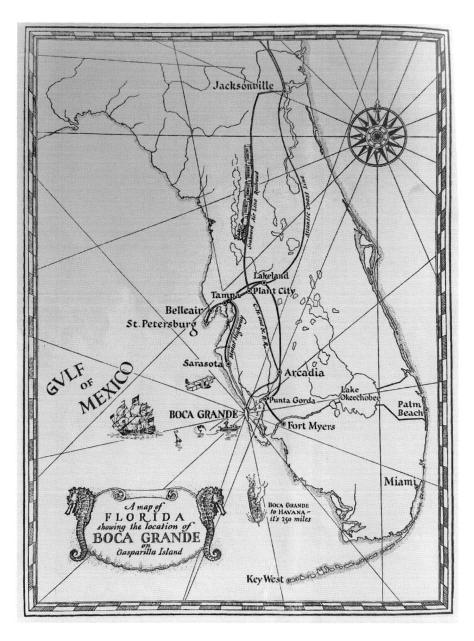

A Florida map from a 1927 sales brochure shows the way to Gasparilla Island and Boca Grande. *Author's collection.*

ACKNOWLEDGEMENTS

First, foremost and out of self-preservation, I thank my darling wife, Sally Stewart, for keeping me on an even keel during this two-year adventure. Her love and encouragement, not to mention her editing skills as a top-flight journalist, made this book better.

I'm also grateful for the support of my University of Florida mentor, Professor Jean Chance, who taught me how to write and organize my thoughts. Then she performed the selfless act of the first read and offered her critique.

And I want to thank my son, Cheyenne. He was the impetus for this book, because I wanted him to know about the history of his crazy fishing family.

No one put in more time on this labor of love than my editors, Joe Gartrell and Rick Delaney, who were in the boat with me and crushed it when crunch time came at the finish line.

This may be my story about the Fishin' Futches, but so many Gasparilla Islanders close to my heart contributed to preserving a slice of island life.

Becky Seale Paterson's *Pirate Coast Magazine* was the seed for this book, and I thank her for allowing me to cull from stories I wrote for my friend from 2003 to 2007. Many more tales are hidden treasures from my family's chest of secrets.

History is a collaborative effort, and the folks at the Boca Grande Historical Society put in endless hours searching their archives for pictures and information. James and Rose Marie Blaha and Kim Kyle did much of the heavy lifting, but there was invaluable support from members Pam Heilman, Pat Agles, Karen Grace and Betsy Fugate Joiner.

One of my dearest friends, Betsy, is the only native islander among the aforementioned group. The rest hail from somewhere else and love Gasparilla Island as much as anyone who's been here long enough to remember Captain Sam Whidden and his monkey, Chico.

Families shared their photographs and stories, none more so than my cousin and the funniest man alive, William "Dumplin'" Wheeler III. His tales of heroism on the high seas are sprinkled throughout.

I want to thank my friends and island second sons, Bob Morris and Randy Wayne White, for their support. They were my colleagues at the *Fort Myers News-Press* when we covered unbridled growth in the 1970s and '80s in the fastest-growing county in America by telling stories about a vanishing Florida.

Bob's column was called "True Floridians and Other Passing Attractions." A lot of attractions have disappeared, but here's hoping that true Floridians and new Floridians alike enjoy this view of the past as much as I enjoyed writing it.

And I can never forget my old pal Scott Johnson, an extraordinary boatman and storyteller who was there to show me and everyone else where to find the good times. His imprint on this book, like his life, is there between the lines.

Last and most important, my heart goes out to my late brother, Captain Mark Futch, who was bigger than life and left us too early. He told me that if I didn't write about the Futch impact on Boca Grande, good and bad, it would be lost forever.

I couldn't let that happen.

INTRODUCTION

Some folks might say this book about Gasparilla Island and Boca Grande is revisionist history. Whoppers. Nothing but fish stories.

Others might say the truth is there somewhere if you squint your eyes. A third group of believers might swear, "That's the gospel. My granddaddy told me that story the same way."

Each side can be right, and so can I. That's because this is my take based on many sources, some on target, some with nothing in the quiver.

This is what I know about Gasparilla Island, beginning with the ruthless Calusa, who beheaded their enemies; to the conquistadors, who wiped them out; to the Crowninshields, who imported kindness when they stepped off their private train car.

I expect my cousin Captain Dumplin' Wheeler will say, "That ain't how it happened." That's because that's what he says whenever anyone tells a story about the island. Then, in the next sentence, Dumplin' will recite pretty much the same story—except that, according to him, the tarpon's bigger, the stakes are higher and Dumplin's heroism, of course, is more laudable.

This is a love letter to Boca Grande and old Florida. It's about how things used to be on Boca Grande before the world discovered this island of the mind, as artist Jack Barndollar called Gasparilla.

Serious to comedic describes my approach to these whispers and folk tales.

Pirates plundered merchant ships offshore in the 1820s. At the same time, fishing ranchos on Gasparilla and Cayo Costa Islands exported hundreds of thousands of pounds of salted fish to Cuba every year.

William "Dumplin'" Wheeler of Deja Vu Charters can't wait to tell tall tales to his clients as he heads to Cabbage Key. *Author's collection.*

My family, the Fishin' Futches, came ashore in the 1880s to work the ranchos. A dozen years later, my great-grandfather Frank Futch figured out how to catch tarpon on a rod and reel and started the guide-fishing industry on the southwest Florida coast.

Gasparilla Island rum smugglers, like my grandfather Dan Futch, thumbed their noses at the law in the 1920s. A half century later, sons of sons of sailors carried on Boca Grande's smuggling tradition by importing tons of marijuana through Boca Grande Pass.

Rich or poor, longtime natives embraced the island's reputation as a shelter for runaways in search of an escape at the end of the line.

Some anecdotes are culled from historical pieces written for Becky Paterson's *Pirate Coast Magazine*. Others originated with my time as editor of the weekly *Gasparilla Gazette*. Still others came from Boca Grande Historical Society records. Many originated with conversations and interviews with islanders who experienced a different time and place.

Then there are the stories based on yarns passed down through four generations of Futches.

Both sides of my family are "True Floridians," according to writer Bob Morris, himself a True Floridian from Leesburg who has spent many dog days on the island.

Not long after Florida became a state in 1845, my great-great-great-grandfather John Roberts of Green Turtle Cay, Bahamas, landed in Key West and offered his skills as a ship's caulker.

My great-grandfather Frank Futch was born in 1866 at Pinellas Point, south St. Petersburg. In 1883, he married the former Sarah Melissa Slaughter, sailed to Gasparilla Island and fished for Peacon's Ranch at the north end.

Long before the Futches, the Calusa Indians ruled southwest Florida for one thousand years. The boundaries and breadbasket of their kingdom stretched from the Peace River, which empties into Charlotte Harbor, to the Caloosahatchee River, which feeds Pine Island Sound near Fort Myers to the Everglades.

Gargantuan people, Calusa men measured more than six feet tall, some approaching seven. They feasted on oysters and sacrificed their enemies, sticking severed heads on poles outside their lodges and at spots along the boundaries of Calusa land.

But the Calusa were no match for Spanish explorer Hernando de Soto and his brutal army. They landed on Gasparilla and neighboring islands in the 1500s. The Calusa were wiped out with lead shot and disease by the end of the 1700s.

As Spain's power ebbed and the conquistadors disappeared, pirate José Gaspar and his buccaneers ruled Charlotte Harbor. As legend goes, Gasparilla Island's namesake imprisoned women, including Spanish princess Josefa, while he plundered merchant ships in the Gulf of Mexico.

In 1821, American naval ships disguised as commercial vessels lured in Gaspar, then sank his sloop as Gaspar lashed himself to the anchor and went over the side.

It's a helluva legend, and my family likes thinking it's true. Maybe. Maybe not. Doesn't matter. A José Gaspar story never fails to entertain.

And that's what you're going to get here—intriguing stories about buccaneers and rum smugglers, marijuana kingpins who were twentieth-century pirates, tarpon fishermen and fisherwomen and the scions of industry who turned Boca Grande into their winter playground.

Even Goldfinger has a part as a Gasparilla Island player.

As an added attraction, an island recipe at the end of each chapter provides a thread of connection to that chapter.

I hope this collection of fish tales brings smiles to longtime islanders who remember taking the ferry.

If you're new to Boca Grande, this is what happened on this spit of sand before and after a bridge to the mainland opened in 1958. The hope is that after reading these stories, natives and newbies alike will think, "I'll be darned. I didn't know that."

I love Boca Grande. It's in my heart and blood.

For more than a century, there were so many Futches on Boca Grande that the locals liked to say, "Shake a tree and a Futch will fall out." Most of those fallen Futches would get up, dust themselves off and tell you a story.

Like I'm going to do right now.

—David Futch
Fourth-generation Boca Grande raconteur and fishing guide

1

A PIRATE IN THE STRAITS

Prohibition never stopped Dan Futch from doing what he had to do to put food on the table.

The law meant nothing to him, because there wasn't much law around when Futch set out on treacherous trips across the Florida Straits to smuggle Cuban rum. Canadian whiskey and champagne were big sellers— whatever he could trade for American cigarettes.

Every summer from 1924 to 1932, my grandfather made a familiar run to Cárdenas, Cuba. On one trip, life and death were at play. But the prospect of trouble never fazed Futch, because he'd been in plenty of scrapes in his short twenty-six years.

As in previous trips, Futch hired the same man in Cardenas to watch his boat, *Sweeney*, and help him load it with one hundred wood boxes of contraband. As the man handed down case after case from the dock, Futch noticed the helper eyeing the new outboard motor clipped to the stern in case his inboard engine failed, like it did the last time.

As Futch prepared to depart, he grabbed a pipe wrench at his feet, just in case. As the helper tossed the last line on to the boat, he attempted to snatch the new outboard motor off the stern of the twenty-six-foot open boat. Futch struck the would-be thief in the head with the wrench, sending him face-first into the gin-clear water.

Futch hadn't come this far to let someone take his four-horsepower Elto Evinrude. On his last run, Futch had broken down in the Gulf Stream, drifting north for three days until he fixed the motor somewhere off Miami Beach.

My grandfather and rum smuggler, Daniel Webster Futch, with Grandma Nellie, and unidentified child during a tarpon outing. *Courtesy of the Futch family.*

The stinging memory of suffering in the sun made him resolve that it wasn't going to happen again, now that he had that Elto.

Pulling away from the Cardenas dock, Futch turned to see another dockworker jump in and pull the man out. Police would arrive soon enough, and too much was at stake: the booze, the boat and his freedom. Positive that justice wasn't going to be on the side of an American in Cuba—especially one whose boat was loaded to the gills with illegal liquor—he shoved the throttle into the corner and headed to Key West.

As Futch put it, "This weren't no time to stick around to see if he was dead."

Every summer for nearly a decade, Futch followed a familiar route from Gasparilla Island to Key West, then ninety miles across the fickle Florida Straits.

Futch motored the *Sweeney* down the coast, passing Fort Myers Beach and Naples. At Caxambas, south of Marco Island, he cut across Florida Bay to Key West, where it was a straight shot to the Pearl of the Caribbean. Same for the return: Across the straits and up the Florida Keys before hugging the Ten Thousand Islands—a good place to hide with help from his friend, Totch Brown, the celebrated rum and pot smuggler who lived in that maze of mangroves.

Dan Futch with wife, Nellie, during World War II in Mayport near Jacksonville, where he captained a tug to push battleships around for the navy. *Courtesy of Mark and Kathy Futch.*

Before a trip, Futch would rig *Sweeney* to carry as much as possible, nailing two-by-ten-inch planks to the gunwale to create more freeboard, then loading it with cases of American cigarettes.

When he arrived in Cuba, Futch might wait days to trade cigarettes for rum. During the downtime, he'd venture to Havana. "It was beautiful. The horseshoe harbor all lit up. And the prettiest whores I've ever seen."

But on this occasion, he was in a hurry. The floater he left behind would be of interest to the cops. Futch shoved off with one hundred cases of rum demijohns, each carrying two one-gallon glass jugs encased in wicker.

Prohibition didn't stop people from drinking. The landed gentry on the beach were accustomed to the Roaring Twenties, which meant their generosity offered Futch a good living.

Boca Grande's white sand beaches attracted the upper crust, who traveled south to Gasparilla Island in private railroad cars.

By the time Dan Futch made his first smuggling run in 1924, the wealthiest of those in the *Social Register* needed liquid courage to fuel a blur of dances, parties and picnics. Futch was happy to oblige.

In a 2003 Boca Grande Historical Society *Connections* story by Malabar Hornblower, Du Pont scion and Gasparilla Inn owner Bayard Sharp said: "Before liquor became legal, parties ran on spirits supplied by four or five fishermen. Nobody considered it a crime. One or two would go to Cuba. When the cargo was brought in, they would divide it and run it over to one of the islands around Useppa. Each guy had his own place to bury the booze and would bring it up as the demand rose."

Some of the ill-gotten liquor was set aside for customers in northern cities. After a conductor received his cut, the hooch was hidden in the bottom of iced-down barrels of fish loaded onto the Charlotte Harbor & Northern Railway (CH&N), eventually making its way to New York City.

But most jugs found a home on Boca Grande, and money flowed into Futch's pockets.

On every trip to Cuba, Futch daydreamed about an eight-cylinder Hudson Great Eight coupe he desired. "Because back then if you had a Hudson, you was somebody," Futch said in a 1980 interview a few months before he died.

Whenever Futch held court on a dock, any dock, he crouched like a baseball catcher. Sometimes, he wore cheap canvas deck shoes. More often, he'd be barefoot in his guide outfit: a pair of khaki pants and a khaki shirt from a Sears-Roebuck catalogue. An ever-present nonfilter Pall Mall cigarette hung from his lips as he talked, the bill of his baseball cap always tilted up in defiance.

The skin on the back of his neck was crosshatched and the color of an old saddle, the result of spending every day in the sun.

Futch and his brothers were tough guys. They had to be in order to carve out an existence on an island where the local fishermen joked, "The mosquitoes are so big they can screw a turkey standing flat-footed."

One thing Futch knew for sure: smuggling was the only way he was ever going to get ahead—or that new Hudson.

Futch's brother Rayford "Sugar Boy" Futch followed him to Cuba in search of riches.

Even though there was big money in smuggling, fishing was the island's bread-and-butter industry. Grueling, grimy work, the men stood waist-deep in brackish water all day pulling on heavy cotton nets coated with tar meant to keep unwanted critters like crabs from eating the line. Rattlesnakes and stingrays were a constant threat. On the other hand, smuggling was the gravy on the biscuit of life.

To the Futches, fishing and smuggling went hand in hand—family businesses, with plenty of them up to the task.

Dan and his seven brothers and three sisters went shoeless most of the time growing up. Life was hard and cruel. They watched Sammy die of influenza at age sixteen. Oscar stepped on a catfish spine and passed a few days later from blood poisoning. Little Rosa left us when she was a baby.

The rest of the Futches stuck together out of survival. There was Albert (who went by "Ab"), Lela, Charlie ("Dunk"), Nathaniel ("Nat"), Robert ("Brick"), Elonzo ("Lonnie"), Rayford, Daniel ("Dan") and, finally, the baby, Connie. Dunk had a son whom no one called by his first name—he's always been Pork Chop.

In the winter, when nor'westers made it too dangerous to cross the Florida Straits, Dan Futch operated a private yacht for Edgar Moss, nephew of Al Capone. Later, Moss succeeded Uncle Al when the mobster was jailed for tax evasion. Dan even caddied for Moss, once having to chase down a thief guilty of stealing Moss's golf shoes from a locker at the Biltmore in Coral Gables. "It was his ass or mine."

Moss loved Boca Grande, mostly because he could get away from Miami. Moss also liked Kim Johnson's backwater gambling casino and speakeasy immediately east of the Gasparilla Inn Golf Course.

Where the end of Fourth Street met Boca Grande Bayou, gamblers climbed the arching Japanese Bridge, then cut east across the course to the casino, built on stilts over the water.

At night, Johnson's juke joint jumped. Blue bloods and fishermen rubbed shoulders, boozed, tossed dice and played cards. As Dan Futch put it, "At Kim Johnson's, you couldn't tell the difference between the fishing guides and the rich people who lived on the beach. Both sides getting drunk and acting silly."

Thirsty beachfronters kept Futch sailing back and forth the 250 miles between Gasparilla and Cuba. Getting there was a matter of dead reckoning. Educated guesswork using a compass combined with a healthy respect for the Gulf Stream's unpredictable nature and shifting currents.

In the ninety-mile stretch between Key West and Cuba, four billion cubic feet of water rushes through the Florida Straits every second. Futch made five or six trips a summer, almost never in winter, because of howling nor'westers. "If you had good weather, it would take about five days from Boca Grande to get down, five days to get back," he said. "The money was good, so we didn't have no reason to hurry. The number of trips depended on how much a man wanted to make. It was a lot better than being a tarpon guide making $10 a day."

There were a couple of close calls when *Sweeney* was overloaded. In a 1980 interview, my grandfather told me he was spotted at night off Caxambas by a patrol boat manned by federal revenuers.

They shot at me but never came close. They followed me for a long time but I was so damned far ahead I snuck into them waters where the Ten-Thousand Islands meets the Everglades at Lost Man River. They couldn't find me. I knew the waters and they didn't.

Another time I fooled 'em when I was near Duck Key near Marathon half way down the Florida Keys. I pulled into Duck Key with my running lights off. Then I raced for the other side of one of them little islands that was nearby and turned my lights back on. The patrol boats come racing toward me and they run aground on the island I was hidin' behind. I took off in my boat runnin' and laughin' my ass off at them.

Each time he returned to Boca Grande, thirsty customers were waiting. "Cars come in from all over the United States, mostly from Chicago," Futch recalled. "I sold a lot of it to people in Boca Grande. Made plenty of money.

"The rich people living on the beach was all drunks but was also good people. They took care of the commercial fishermen and their families. They built the school, the churches, they loaned us money. If they chartered you to take them tarpon fishing and the wind was blowin' so you couldn't go out, they paid you anyway."

But nothing lasts forever. After years of smuggling, Treasury Department investigators had Dan Futch in their crosshairs, but it had nothing to do with rum. The feds suspected Futch of being in league with the infamous Albury brothers, who had been arrested in Miami. The government charged the Alburys with murdering four federal agents after the agents boarded their boat and found illegal immigrants.

Futch had a good alibi. He was one hundred miles away when the Alburys committed the deed. The feds knew about Futch being in cahoots with the brothers on a previous rum-running operation and thought he was involved this time.

Futch told the feds he didn't know diddly about the murders. They didn't care and threw Futch in a Tampa jail, where they questioned him for three days before releasing him with a cut lip and a bruised back from an "interrogation." "That's when I realized there is no justice…and there never was."

The Albury brothers didn't fare so well. Following a brief trial, a circuit-riding judge found them guilty, pronounced the sentence and ordered them to be hanged immediately from the rafters of a Dinner Key airplane hangar next to Biscayne Bay.

Futch was scared straight and never smuggled again. "And like I told them revenuers in Tampa, I never smuggled people. I only smuggled liquor 'cause rum bottles don't talk. Men do."

EL FLORIDITA DAIQUIRI

The old Pink Elephant used to make a version of the El Floridita Daiquiri originally concocted at Havana's famed El Floridita bar, where Ernest Hemingway preferred to drink. A sign behind the bar reads, "La Cuna del Daiquiri," which translates to "birthplace of the daiquiri."

This is not a frozen drink made in a blender. It's shaken, not stirred. Sometimes, it's thrown, but that takes practice. In the old days at El Floridita, the concoction was "thrown" through the air from one stainless-steel shaker to one made of glass—something about mixing the rum with air to bring out hidden flavor.

Here's how it's still done at El Floridita:

Fill a glass tumbler with ice. Pour in two or three ounces of Appleton White rum or Matusalem Platino or even a light rum like Mount Gay Eclipse from Barbados.

Add simple syrup (one or two tablespoons), then one ounce of key lime or Persian lime juice and one tablespoon of Peter Heering Cherry Liqueur.

Make a seal over the glass tumbler with one of stainless steel and shake until the steel tumbler is frosty.

Strain into a chilled martini glass, rim with a wheel of lime and toast Dan Futch for smuggling the rum and recipe back to Boca.

2
SQUARE GROUPER

Prohibition provided a steady income for Depression-era fishermen willing to smuggle liquor.

But the booze-trafficking cash cow abruptly ended in 1933, when Congress repealed the Eighteenth Amendment, making alcohol legal again.

Thirty years later, sons of sons of sailors invigorated Boca Grande's underground economy when they brought a new sophistication to smuggling. This time around, Gasparilla Island fishermen focused on importing marijuana.

Night-vision goggles and single-sideband radios became standard issue for modern-day pot smugglers.

Starting in the mid-1960s, several islanders seized the opportunity to sail burlap-wrapped forty-pound bales of pot nicknamed "square grouper" through Boca Grande Pass.

Fishing guides involved in the illegal trade also learned a new trick. Instead of hiding their ill-gotten gains under a mattress, they buried cash in paraffin-coated PVC pipes so the money wouldn't turn to mush underground.

For the first time in their lives, a band of island fishermen could afford to buy things they had only dreamed about.

Home ownership was within reach—at the least, a down payment on one. Fishermen were able to put their children through college so that their offspring wouldn't have to pull on nets for a living or end up in dead-end jobs like washing and ironing clothes for wealthy tourists staying at the Gasparilla Inn. That's what my grandma Nellie Futch did for decades out of the laundry in the back of Mickle Apartments, now Hotel H.

Discretion made smuggling possible. Spending the money required secrecy and planning. Nothing flashy. Buy things in drips and drabs so as not to draw attention. Cash always brought better bargaining power when haggling over a new boat engine or truck.

First, a history of how fishermen struggled before their sons and grandsons smuggled so much pot they ran out of space to bury their money.

After rum smuggling petered out, Boca Grande fishermen like Dan Futch fell on hard times. Gasparilla Island fishermen scratched out an existence making ten dollars a day guiding for tarpon in the summer then netting mullet for a nickel a pound in winter.

The gravy was gone. No more expensive Hudson cars in the driveway, like the one Dan Futch had to sell when the well dried up.

Years of struggle marked the lean times before World War II broke out and the island went dark. No lights at night, which meant no fishing after sundown or before dawn, when tarpon bite the best.

All able-bodied men were called to duty. Since most were boatmen, they served in the U.S. Navy, Coast Guard or Merchant Marine.

One islander with no sea legs at all became its biggest hero.

Weighing in at 140 pounds soaking wet, master carpenter and tank driver for General George Patton, my uncle Jack Silcox was awarded the Silver Star for gallantry in action near Albersbach, Germany.

During a fierce battle, Silcox covered four hundred yards of open terrain to retrieve pinned-down wounded soldiers, loading them onto and into his Sherman tank and bringing them to safety. Then Silcox went back again, returning with medical supplies and picking up more wounded comrades.

With victory over the Axis powers, island heroes returned, and Boca boomed. Winter residents and tourists again flocked to the island to fish and play golf. Life returned to a solitary and insular existence. Boats and trains were the only ways to get here.

Then a bridge to the mainland opened in 1958, allowing easier access to shopping in the big cities of Punta Gorda, Venice and Sarasota.

People were no longer flocking to the island as they once did, while plenty of longtime islanders decided to flock off.

By the mid-1960s, Boca Grande was in shambles. Ignored, the iconic train depot deteriorated as termites ate timbers and beams. Falling roof tiles made walking underneath dangerous. Depot windows became targets for rock-throwing island boys.

Fisher families like the Futches, Lowes, Padillas and Joiners lived on Whitewash Alley, the first name for Tarpon Avenue. Wives mended nets in the front yards of "shotgun" homes. As natives moved off the island in the late 1960s, one of those homes could be had for a paltry $8,000.

Whitewash Alley homes weren't the only ones showing wear and tear. Beachfront mansions fell into disrepair. Nor'westers blowing off the Gulf ravaged the Newberry estate on Gilchrist Avenue between Fourth and Third Streets. Alexander Calder's beachfront estate at the end of Fourth Street on the beach fared no better. Rolf and Ingrun Wagschal spent years and a minor fortune renovating the great artist's estate. Even the grand home, Las Olas, at the end of First Street, seemed long in the tooth after years of neglect following Louise Crowninshield's death in 1958.

Boca Grande was no longer "on the Upp and Upp," as the sign over the bait tank at Whidden's Marina claimed.

The island needed an economic boost and got it when an exploding market for marijuana ushered in a new way of life for fisher families in dire need. The drumbeat was on, and the Woodstock generation adopted marijuana as a way of thumbing its collective nose at anyone over thirty.

In the 1960s, most of the pot coming to America originated in Mexico via Texas and the interstate highway system. Some came from Jamaica, but it was spotty. The only thing available was Mexican "ragweed" that lacked kick.

That all changed when South and Central American pot growers hooked up with Florida smugglers whose families had experience with importing illegal goods. Several Gasparilla Island fishermen were recruited for the burgeoning business. Why not? One nighttime run offshore to a waiting ship paid $15,000 in 1970 money.

Smuggling returned to Boca Grande, the island's remote location a plus to modern-day pirates.

A resourceful Boca Grande fishing guide and a Key West sailor recognized the potential and stepped up to form a new age of sophisticated smugglers. They weren't intent on running offshore to a ship and picking up a ton or so for someone else. They wanted their own ship so they could make millions, not peanuts. With a benefactor who was willing to buy a boat and put up the money for the pot and the equipment, they were ready to go for throttle up.

The island guide and his sailor pal started buying up the necessary gadgets, employing the same stealth used by U.S. Navy Seals. Handy tools like single-sideband radios enabled worldwide communications, specifically calls to South America. Night-vision scopes offered a decided advantage when slinking around Charlotte Harbor on a moonless night.

But they didn't always rely on the pitch black of a new moon to sneak stuff through. Even high noon was a good time to smuggle. It took chutzpah, a trait the Boca Grande gang owned in spades.

Super Bowl Sunday was optimum for bringing in the goody. They figured everyone would be watching the game, including Marine Patrol officers charged with patrolling Charlotte Harbor.

Start to finish, here's how the plan came together every time. Well, almost every time.

From the moment the Key West sailor departed Colombia until his marijuana-packed sailboat arrived in Boca Grande Pass, the fishing guide stayed in touch via a single-sideband radio.

For local and national calls to the leader of the pack and other members of the eight-man team, the guide never used a landline unless it was a phone booth, the smart play, because the law didn't tap them. "I put a lot of quarters in the pay phones that used to be on Millers Marina dock and the ones next to the post office," said the Boca Grande fishing guide who was in charge of offloading and hiring five other fishermen to help.

In addition to the Boca Grande guide and the Key West sailor, the new entrepreneurs included the boss, a cowboy-boot-wearing Spaniard who called himself Joe. No one was ever sure if that was his real name. For that matter, no one knew anyone's real name. For years, each gang member owned an alias. In the event of a bust, nobody knew how to identify the others. Expert marksmen, they poked fun at themselves by dubbing their band of buccaneers "The Gang That Couldn't Shoot Straight," a nod to the Jimmy Breslin book about inept mafia.

Joe the Spaniard financed the entire operation by first paying a Guajiro Indian in Colombia to grow acres of marijuana.

The Conch sailor was recruited not just for his sailing skills. He had another role to play. Joe cast the Conch as an aristocrat cruising the high seas.

The sailor trimmed his hair and beard, then traded in his shorts, Hawaiian shirt and flip-flops for white bell-bottom pants, a blue-and-white-striped Breton chemise favored by French sailors and Sperry Topsider deck shoes. His favorite part of the costume was his jacket with epaulets.

Should a patrol boat make an appearance while he was on the high seas, the sailor completed the illusion by firing up his hand-carved meerschaum pipe. Nothing to see here. "We were acting as Brits sailing under British papers," the Conch captain said. "The boat had dual registry in the U.S. and the Isle of Man. The first time we did the deed we were followed by a Coast Guard helicopter ship for six hours until I reached the oil platforms off New Orleans.

"Twice I sailed through a NATO fleet. There was some serious rectal puckering going on when a British Navy ship pulled alongside. But I lit my pipe and looked the part and they left me alone."

Before the sailboat would depart Riohacha, Colombia, farmhands jammed tons of reefer into the captain's fifty-two-foot Laurent Giles yawl.

On other occasions, the Gang used bigger sailboats capable of taking on more "square grouper." "The boats of choice for us were the Winnebagos of the sailing world like a big Irwin or a 50-to-60-foot 'leaky Tiki' made in Taiwan. The Laurent Giles wood boat was used once, but the mass-produced fiberglass boats like the Irwins looked more innocent and common and that's why we liked them."

Bales of pot reached to the ceiling in every cabin as well as in the lazarette, the head and the forecastle. On the other hand, the salon and galley were left empty in the event the Coast Guard wanted to take a quick look without boarding.

The circuitous run from the northeast coast of Colombia to Gasparilla Island took ten days. The captain started out heading northwest toward the Yucatán, where he'd make a northerly turn to lose himself among dozens of oil platforms off Louisiana. When he felt safe, he tacked southeast to the Boca Grande Pass bell buoy, where the Boca Grande fishing guide came aboard. "It was my idea to sail into Boca Grande Pass on Sunday in the middle of the day," the Conch sailor said. "Better to smuggle right in front of the law instead of behind their backs. Then we'd anchor up in the harbor and wait for nightfall."

A couple hours after sunset, the Boca Grande fishing guide took the helm. He headed east to the far side of Charlotte Harbor, where he was met by an offloading crew of net fishermen, each receiving the standard rate of $15,000 for one night's work—more than they'd make during a three-month mullet-netting season.

The Gang always hooked up at a place called Two Pines, a middle-of-nowhere spot south of Burnt Store Road that had been a favorite of smugglers since Prohibition. The only things around were pine trees, palmettos and a dirt road ending at the Charlotte Harbor shoreline.

A couple of days before the sailboat's arrival, the Boca Grande fishing guide dragged a forty-foot engineless barge to Two Pines, where he shoved it into a hidey-hole encircled by mangroves and containing two one-room huts on stilts, where the Gang would lie in wait for the sailboat.

As the tarpon guide proudly said, "I once took my seven-year-old son with me to hide the scow before the sailboat got here. I guess that makes him the world's youngest smuggler. Like the country western song says, 'It's a family tradition.'"

After offloading the tightly packed sailboat using crowbars to loosen the load, the crew stacked bales twenty feet high onto the barge. Then the Gang pushed and dragged the gray scow to shore, where waiting rental trucks were backed up to the shoreline about a mile south of Burnt Store Marina.

The smuggling operation worked like a well-oiled machine, except for the last trip, with their biggest load at stake. In the aftermath of a heavy thunderstorm, the dirt road to the shoreline turned to soup, and the rental trucks bogged down in mud. Daylight was coming, and they needed to get the hell out of there.

The Gang spent an hour cutting down pine trees with chainsaws to build a log road over water-soaked ground. During that time, the fishing guide took a fast skiff to Boca Grande to get a Jeep to pull out the trucks.

The chainsaw noise during tree-trimming ratcheted up the paranoia of seven men praying for a four-wheel drive but waiting for red-and-blue flashing lights from cop cars patrolling Burnt Store Road.

Two hours before sunup, the guide returned and secured six-inch-wide nylon straps from the Jeep to the trucks. With encouragement from several strong men pushing, the trucks broke free.

At first light, as the muddied trucks approached him, a lookout along Burnt Store Road stood and signaled the all clear. No one was driving the deserted two-lane blacktop.

Weighted down with tons of square grouper, two drivers made their way to Pine Island Road, then fifteen miles to US 41. Always two trucks, always splitting off so if police stopped one, they wouldn't get the other.

The drivers met up again at a Tamiami Trail motel to wash splattered mud off the trucks and themselves. A swift goodbye, and like that, the trucks disappeared, their cargo areas bloated with high-grade marijuana.

After crossing the Caloosahatchee Bridge, one driver turned left to connect with State Road 80 in downtown Fort Myers. Next stop, West Palm Beach, then I-95 south to Miami, the hub of the East Coast drug world.

Mercury Marquis cars with heavy-duty shock absorbers ferried eight hundred pounds each up the I-95 corridor to New York and Boston. Anyone who smoked a joint at Harvard University in the 1980s can thank the Gang That Couldn't Shoot Straight.

The other driver headed south to Naples on US 41, aka the Tamiami Trail, then east on Alligator Alley to Miami and up I-95 to Fort Lauderdale, where bales were stored in a safe house that Joe owned off Las Olas Boulevard. In one instance, a buyer walked through the house inspecting the product in the canal-front home and said, "Throw in the house and I'll take everything in it." All six thousand pounds at $400 a pound: $2.4 million in cash.

"We smuggled 28 tons over a four-year period. At an average wholesale price of $400 a pound, that comes to $22 million and change," the Boca Grande fishing guide said. "Joe financed the operation, so he got most of the money, but I rolled my $25,000 fee over on one trip to the next one and made $250,000. We smuggled a lot of pot but we never smuggled cocaine. We considered it bad juju."

Three things gave the Gang the upper hand in getting away with it all: technology, the Boca Grande guide's knowledge of local waters and playing it low-key by never flashing money around.

The fishing guide offered something he had learned from the failings of other smugglers: "None of us spent the money like those guys down in Everglades City who'd smuggle some pot and spend it on new cars and gold watches.

"It's no wonder they went to jail. The Collier County cops had to be wondering why a bunch of mullet fishermen had new Cadillac cars in front of their single-wide trailers."

The Gang's enterprise came to a halt in 1990 but gave the guide a second act. "I started smuggling because I needed the money," the guide said.

I was young and had a family and had just gotten my guide license. I was running someone else's boat and spinning my wheels trying to make a living, every day falling behind.

After all was said and done, I walked away with a quarter-million dollars from the last operation we ever did. I tried to spend it wisely on things like my family, my house, my fishing equipment. I paid for my kids' college.

I didn't want to be like those guys in Everglades City who spent money on silly stuff like Rolex watches. The only watch I ever owned was a $20 Timex I bought at Fugate's Drug Store. The guys in Everglades City rubbed that money in the cops' faces and it cost them. They lost everything and went to prison.

Despite the dangers, the pirate/fishing guide admitted that the thrill of smuggling topped all the cash he buried in his backyard. "I felt alive. I was taking control of my life. I rolled the dice and won.

"After a while when you've got enough money, smuggling becomes all about the giddy-up. The adrenaline rush of getting away with it is indescribable."

The Boca Grande guide and the Conch sailor slipped into anonymity with smiles on their faces and tubes of money in the backyard.

Blonde Brownies

If you don't get the inside joke as to why this brownie recipe is in a story about marijuana, then you missed the 1960s.

In its heyday a half century ago, Doris Wheeler, Betsy Joiner and my aunt Edith Silcox, wife of Jack the war hero, and their daughters, Becky and Jackie Silcox, would take turns roaming the old Pink Elephant dining room carrying a silver tray filled with chocolate and blonde brownies. They were free, and you were allowed one each. Diners in the know would pass on the chocolate ones and grab two of its chewy, golden cousins that melted in your mouth. They're easy to make and a dream to eat.

Ingredients:
¼ cup melted butter
1 cup light brown sugar
1 egg, beaten
1 teaspoon vanilla
½ cup all-purpose flour
Salt
1 teaspoon double-acting baking powder
Chopped walnuts or pecans
(Marijuana optional)

Mix first four ingredients in a large bowl. In a separate bowl, sift ½ cup all-purpose flour, a pinch of salt and 1 teaspoon double-acting baking powder. Slowly stir the butter/sugar mixture into the flour mixture, then stir in ½ to 1 cup of chopped walnuts or pecans. Pour into a 9-by-9-inch pan coated with cooking spray.

Bake for 20 to 25 minutes at 350 degrees.

3

SISTER ISLANDS

Gasparilla Island's sisters surround it, essential pieces of Boca Grande's backstory.

How did Gasparilla Island get its name? The answer is wrapped in a myth.

In the early 1900s, at the age of nearly 100, Juan "Panther Key John" Gomez bent a lot of ears with his claims of serving as cabin boy for the cutthroat pirate José Gaspar. For a small donation, Gomez would regale tourists and fishermen with tales of Gasparilla Island's namesake.

But according to anthropologist André-Marcel d'Ans, Gasparilla Island appears on maps before José Gaspar was born, Gasparilla Island likely taking its name from Spanish missionary Gasparillo.

As d'Ans writes in a story for the University of South Florida publication *Scholar Commons* (December 1, 1980), "Pirate Jose Gaspar, alias Gasparilla, never existed. This fact is proven both by the absence of his name in the Spanish and American archives and by the total absence of any material trace of his presence in Florida. There are no ruins that might be attributed to him and not a single coin from his fabulous treasure has ever been found."

No one likes that story. Or the one about missionary man Friar Gasparillo, who ministered to Spanish and Cuban fishermen and "for whom Gasparilla Island and northern inlet, Gasparilla Pass, were named on maps of 1760–63. It is certain that Gaspar was not a pirate as romantics like to believe," wrote Punta Gorda historian Lindsey Williams on his blog lindseywilliams.org.

Despite evidence to the contrary, José Gaspar's tale of piracy and captive women has long legs.

"Panther Key John" claimed to have met Napoleon at age five, wherein the emperor patted him on the head as he stood in a parade route. That was the bait, then John reeled you in with yarns about the ruthless and bloodthirsty Gaspar. Tourists weren't the only ones Gomez fleeced.

Gasparilla Island developers also fell for Gomez's pitch. Latching onto the lie, early island developers published a sales brochure in 1927 touting Gaspar's reign of terror.

Tampa's ruling class beat them to the punch by promoting the Gaspar myth when they held the first coronation ball of Gasparilla in 1904. Poof! Illusion became reality at the hands of marketing specialists who spread the José Gaspar fable.

More about the big lie. Born in 1756 in Spain, José Gaspar allegedly served in the Spanish navy until turning to piracy in 1783, plundering the Southwest Florida coast until the USS *Enterprise* dispatched him to Davy Jones's locker in 1821.

Disguised as a merchant vessel, the *Enterprise* lured Gaspar into thinking one last prize on the horizon was there for the taking. When Gaspar approached the faux merchant ship, the navy captain blew him to kingdom come. As his sloop sank, Gaspar wrapped himself in anchor chains and went down with his ship. At least that's the way Panther Key John told it.

The Gaspar legend lives on. Ye Mystic Krewe of Gasparilla held their first parade along the Hillsborough River in downtown Tampa in 1904. In 1911, they borrowed a merchant vessel and decorated it in pirate fashion. The Krewe bought a sloop in 1930 and christened it *Jose Gaspar*, sailing their pirate vessel up the river and bringing the city to its knees for a day. Except for war and the pandemic, Gaspar has been celebrated every January with a full-scale takeover of Tampa. The seven-hundred-member Krewe includes area businessmen dressed in swashbuckling garb tossing beads and firing twenty cannons from the Krewe's upgraded pirate ship, the 147-foot, sail-rigged *Jose Gasparilla*, built for $100,000 in the mid-1950s. Since then, they've upgraded to a 165-footer.

A half-million people watch from the shore as the Krewe unleashes volleys from their galleon, pirates hanging from the yardarms and deckhands threatening the populace.

The José Gaspar myth is a favorite, and so is the story of the first peoples to build an empire on the lower Gulf Coast.

Calusa Indians ruled Southwest Florida for one thousand years until they disappeared in the 1700s. A sophisticated and warring society, the Calusa built pyramids and mounds on Charlotte Harbor and Pine Island Sound keys. These structures resembled the pyramids of their Yucatán ancestors. Like their distant cousins, the Calusa had a mean streak.

Neighboring tribes steered clear of the Calusa for good reason. Calusa kings sent warnings to their enemies by decapitating intruders and sticking their heads on stakes along their borders. The Timucuans wouldn't go near them, calling the Calusa *yathampa* ("bad people").

Manasota Indians and the Tocabagan tribe in the Tampa Bay area never ventured south of Boca Grande Pass. They feared running into the hated Calusa, even though the Tocabagans could be downright inhospitable themselves.

During his exploration of the Charlotte Harbor region in 1513, Ponce de León described the Calusa as tall, some seven feet, their hair piled high to make them look bigger.

Spanish explorer Hernando de Soto had his run-ins with the Calusa, fighting them to a draw. De León—all four feet, eleven inches of him— savaged the Calusa in 1521. One skirmish led to his death. During a battle, de León was mortally wounded by a Calusa arrow. His entourage returned to Havana, where Florida's discoverer died.

Muskets and swords didn't cause the demise of the Calusa. Enslavement and wars with the Creek Nation and Seminoles, capped off by European-borne diseases, wiped out the Calusa by the mid-1700s.

Cubans and Spaniards took over, dominating Charlotte Harbor by creating a fishing industry based on mullet.

CAYO PELAU ("KI-YO PUH-LAU")

Cayo Pelau is Gasparilla Island's nearby sister. Located east and a little north of the Gasparilla Inn Golf Course on the western edge of Bull Bay, Cayo Pelau's white-sand beach and overhanging mangroves make it ideal for snook fishing from a shallow-draft boat.

Beware. Don't step foot on this cursed key.

Some commercial fishermen still refuse to go ashore. Old-timers believe the island to be haunted. At night, when the wind is up, a wailing moan can be heard drifting across Cayo Pelau, the siren's song growing louder as fishermen approach.

More likely, fishermen have been fooled over the years by the sound of wind whistling through a mound of ancient conch shells. It took a millennium for ancient peoples to build the Cayo Pelau midden by tossing aside their trash of hollowed-out horse conchs.

The 126-acre Cayo Pelau was designated a nature preserve in 2007 after Lee County paid Carapilla Corporation $2.5 million for Cayo Pelau Preserve to protect it from treasure hunters. For several years into the late 1990s, gold seekers cut through the shell midden searching for buried pirate booty.

To this day, Cayo Pelau can be a creepy place when horse conchs moan at the moon.

Captain Dumplin' Wheeler of Boca Grande has had his run-ins with Cayo Pelau ghosts. He said in my June 2006 *Pirate Coast Magazine* piece "Cayo Pelau: A Ghost Story":

> *When I was a kid, we all knew Cayo Pelau as "Haunted Island," and it seemed like every time we went over there something strange happened. I've been there when there was rain and lightning like I've never seen. I've heard stories about people fishing there and hands coming over the gunwales of their boats. The old-timers who told me stories about Cayo Pelau were dead serious about what went on there after the sun went down.*
>
> *Those old-timers thought the ghosts were those of Jose Gaspar's pirates. They may have been telling these wild stories because they were storing moonshine there and didn't want anyone snooping around.*

Before the Calusa arrived, early peoples found Charlotte Harbor a fine place to live. Scientists have uncovered ceramic shards dating to 800 BC. The brittle pieces reside in the archives of the Florida Museum of Natural History in Gainesville.

Little is known of the first peoples who inhabited the Charlotte Harbor region. In 10,000 BC, Native Americans lived at Little Salt Spring next to what is now Heron Creek Middle School in nearby North Port. University of Miami researchers at the Rosenstiel School of Marine and Atmospheric Science have proved that early natives who lived at the paleontological site cooked a giant turtle in its shell.

There's some information about Native Americans who put down roots on Cayo Pelau around AD 900, University of Florida archaeologist George Luer said in 2006. "We still don't know what to call them," Luer said. "They had no written language, so there's nothing written about who they were. But because of the barrier of Boca Grande Pass, the Cayo Pelau natives were more aligned with the Cape Haze natives to the north than they were with the Calusa to the south."

In a bygone era, the northern Charlotte Harbor tribes living on Cayo Pelau were subservient to the Calusa. "Everything depended on the ruthlessness of the current Calusa king," said John Worth of the Randell Research Center at Pineland, stewards of Charlotte Harbor Native American archaeological sites. "If the Calusa to the south were stronger, they were given more attention. But if they were weaker, the peoples on the north side of Charlotte Harbor looked north to the Tocabaga Indians, who dominated the Tampa Bay area and were enemies of the Calusa."

The Tocabagans were no slouches when it came to ruthless behavior. "The Spaniards built a fort near present-day Clearwater in 1567," Worth said, "and the Tocabagans killed all the people off the next year."

After the Calusa's demise, an intriguing cast of characters appeared. Starting in the late 1700s and continuing until the mid-1800s, Cayo Pelau inhabitants were a mix of Cuban fishermen and Florida Indians such as the Muspa, as well as the Seminole and Miccosukee tribes, survivors of the Seminole Wars, the longest and most expensive of the Indian wars in America.

By the 1870s, the Cayo Pelau netters had moved to Cayo Costa, where the Padillas from the Canary Islands operated a seine net business. Other fishermen joined Peacon's fish rancho on Gasparilla's north end.

CAYO COSTA

On the south side of Boca Grande Pass, nine-mile-long Cayo Costa could double as a set for the musical *South Pacific*.

In the early 1980s, Lee County bought the uninhabited, three-thousand-acre barrier island and turned it over to the Florida parks system. There are cabins, campsites, dock space and plenty of trails. Johnson Shoals lies to the west, accessible at low tide for virgin shelling opportunities.

The 1870 census revealed that the Santini family of eight was living on Cayo Costa. By 1879, the Santinis were gone, but two fish ranchos remained, one at the south end run by Jose Sega and twenty-six men from Key West, and the other at the north end headed up by Canary Island native Tariva "Captain Pappy" Padilla. Pappy was the sole proprietor, employing twenty-three Spanish and one American fishermen, according to Robert Edic's book *Fisherfolk of Charlotte Harbor, Florida*.

One book in particular, the *Goode Report*, points out the abundance of fish in Charlotte Harbor during the late nineteenth century. Published from 1884 through 1887 by the U.S. Commission of Fish and Fisheries, the book's official title is *The Fisheries and Fishery Industries of the United States* but is unofficially called the *Goode Report* after its author, George Brown Goode, who described the prolific amount of mullet in Charlotte Harbor. "[Mullet] being in immense schools, the upper portions of [the harbor] afford inexhaustible feeding grounds. When leaping from the water in great abundance, mullet make noises like the sound of thunder; this continued day and night."

In 1879, the Sega and Padilla ranchos produced 1,000,000 pounds of salted mullet and 50,000 pounds of dried mullet roe.

In *Fisherfolk*, Edic recounted that a 1900 census put Cayo Costa's population at thirty-nine, most of them Padillas. But there were Colemans and Darnas, who caught, salted, smoked, packed and shipped mullet to Cuba. Tariva would haul his processed fish to Havana and trade for the one thing scarce in Southwest Florida: rum and whiskey.

In 1901, the federal government got wind of Padilla's smuggling operation. Major Peter Leary Jr. and eight men from Key West aboard the USS *MacClane* were sent to Cayo Costa to arrest Padilla and evict his family. By the time Leary arrived, the Padillas were gone. The only trace was a thirty-foot pier and a vegetable garden ripe for the picking.

Once the heat died down, Captain Pappy returned to the island, where he fished until he died in 1910.

Tariva Padilla is buried in the same sandy graveyard on Cayo Costa where dozens of young Cuban boys and men wrapped in sailcloth were laid to rest after drowning in the 1910 hurricane that sank their boats and blew their bodies into Tariva Bayou.

Alfonso "Fonso" Darna was born on Cayo Costa the same year his grandfather Tariva died. The Darnas were the last of the Padillas to leave Cayo Costa in 1958. Most of them moved to Boca Grande, where Fonso lived the rest of his life on Whitewash Alley, hanging and mending nets in his yard.

In his Canary Island patois, Fonso Darna talked with Edic in a 1990 interview about the importance of mullet, with more than one hundred species around the world. "I have always been strictly a mullet fisherman," Darna said during the Edic interview sponsored by the University of Florida's Samuel Proctor Oral History Program. "That's all I ever fished for. Oh, I have fished for pompano and mackerel. Grouper is a good fish. I like mackerel, too. I like any kind of fish. I do not care for redfish too much. In fact, I do not care for them at all. Mullet is all you need."

By the early 1900s, the advent of "fish ice" and rail transportation meant the death knell for salted mullet. The Punta Gorda Fish Company created a system of runboats to service island fishermen with ice and supplies and to pick up their catch. The old ways disappeared. The new business model called for iced fish shipped to northern markets.

Mullet fishermen changed gears and turned their interests to a new industry: recreational sport fishing.

Many of the Cayo Costa netters became tarpon guides, including the Darnas, Colemans, Lowes and Padillas. Fonso's son Merritt "Babe" Darna would become a legendary Boca Grande tarpon guide, along with the likes of Woodrow and Richard Coleman, my uncle Billy Wheeler and his son, William "Dumplin" Wheeler, John "Tater" Spinks and almost any of the Futches. The Joiners out of Whidden's Marina have been a dominant force in tarpon fishing for more than a century.

And Cayo Costa's nearby sister, Cabbage Key, has been a favorite watering hole to guides for nearly eighty years and a hideaway for anyone seeking solitude coupled with a good time.

CABBAGE KEY

East of Cayo Costa and south of Punta Blanca at Intracoastal Marker 60 lies Cabbage Key. The Wells family has run Cabbage Key Inn and Restaurant on the one-hundred-acre shell mound since 1976. It has catered to salty sailors since 1944.

Completed in 1937, Cabbage Key Inn sits atop a thirty-eight-foot Indian midden created over many centuries by Native Americans dumping their trash of oyster, scallop and horse conch shells.

There are six rooms and six cottages decorated in 1940s "island rustic." But visitors don't come to Cabbage for the accommodations. The island is about doing nothing, and plenty of it.

Three cottages, named Rinehart, Tarpon and Doll House, lie at the foot of Cabbage Key's ancient Calusa mound. They have kitchens and run $400 a night. Two cabins without kitchens are $150 a day.

From the dock, a short climb up a path of crushed shells leads to the inn and restaurant, with rooms to let, a bar and large screened-in porches where you can get fresh seafood, a killer cheeseburger and to-die-for key lime pie.

Where you can't remember / What you came to forget...

Cabbage Key is "where you can't remember what you came to forget." *Illustration by Patti Middleton, courtesy Kathy Futch.*

Accessible only by boat, Cabbage Key Inn was built as a home for Alan Rinehart and his wife, Gratia Houghton Rinehart, sister of Arthur Houghton Jr. of Boca Grande and first cousin of actor Katharine Houghton Hepburn.

Gratia's life was a short, mixed bag of happiness and melancholy. Shortly after divorcing Alan Rinehart, son of mystery writer Mary Roberts Rinehart, Gratia contracted breast cancer and died at age thirty-four in 1939. The inn lay fallow for most of World War II, except for tarpon research by the New York Aquarium.

In 1944, artists Larry and Jan Stults bought the island from Gratia's estate. The Stultses spent the next twenty-five years entertaining customers and friends, including labor leader John L. Lewis and crime writer John D. MacDonald, who decompressed after every book by visiting his Sarasota neighbors and bartending at their getaway.

"We weren't even boat or water people," said Larry Stults, ninety years old, during a 1989 interview at his Siesta Key home. "We knew nothing about the hospitality business. We had gone tarpon fishing with Captain Bill Hunter, then took a trip to Captiva. As we passed Cabbage Key, Captain Hunter said it was for sale. Jan and I decided if we don't buy it, someone else will. We used to have notorious house parties."

Cabbage Key, where cheeseburgers in paradise and key lime pie rule. *Courtesy of Cabbage Key.*

The hospitable Rob and Phyllis Wells decided to make a move in 1976 from Piedmont, North Carolina, to Florida. The couple bought Cabbage Key from Bob and Joanne Beck, who bought it from Jimmy Turner after Turner acquired the island from the Stultses in 1969.

Rob and Phyllis Wells's sons are in charge now. Ken runs the resort, while Rob III handles duties at the land-based operation on Pine Island.

Like Temptation Restaurant owners on Boca Grande, the Wells family changed almost nothing. Nor are any changes likely. The funky hideout looks like it always has—an oasis on a hill. "Dad liked Cabbage Key the way it was. He never wanted to change it and we want to uphold his vision," Ken said in November 2018. "We do change some things, but people never notice them."

One improvement became a premier attraction. They added a stairwell to the old water tower next to the inn so that visitors could climb to the top for a panoramic view of surrounding islands.

Cabbage Key continues to be a popular hidey-hole, where you can buy a drink and listen to guests tickle the ivories. "Piano Player Wanted: Good or bad" reads the sign on the upright piano a few steps from the bar.

Singer Neil Young found Cabbage Key to be a good place to disappear. When he was on-island, he preferred being incognito, wearing a Stetson and dark sunglasses and sitting in the bar for hours trading fish stories with strangers. Every so often, bar patrons received a gift when the rock 'n' roll legend sat down at the piano. Young looked familiar, but no one could place him until he belted out "Heart of Gold."

Jimmy Buffett is another rocker who found Cabbage Key. He did so while visiting his sister Laurie McGuane and her husband, writer Thomas McGuane, on Boca Grande. Buffett may not have written "Cheeseburger in Paradise" on the island, but the day the song was released in 1978 on his album *Son of a Son of a Sailor*, Buffett was on his sailboat at Cabbage Key dock. That night at a Fort Myers concert, Buffett dedicated his new song to his new home away from home.

There's an unseen beauty to Cabbage Key. People leave you alone. No one intrudes on your space. The only time anyone lifts an eyebrow is when the son of a son of a sailor puts in and orders a cheeseburger in paradise.

Grandma Nellie Futch's Easy Key Lime Pie

True Floridian Bob Morris once wrote a Fort Myers News-Press *column called True Floridians. In one of those columns, he called my Grandma Nellie's kitchen the finest restaurant in Charlotte County. It didn't matter when you showed up, there was always a table topped with southern fare like fried chicken or mullet, collard greens, baked beans, cornbread and especially pound cake and key lime pie.*

I never saw Grandma Nellie bake one, despite the ingredients calling for egg yolks. She'd put it together and stick it in the refrigerator. I used to do that, but I bake them now, which is probably a good idea because of the egg yolks.

Ingredients
1 pie shell made from graham crackers, melted butter and sugar
2 or 3 egg yolks
3 or 4 ounces of key lime juice
1 14-ounce can of sweetened condensed milk

Place egg yolks in a mixing bowl, add key lime juice and condensed milk and mix thoroughly. Grate in some lime zest for added punch. Pour into shell and bake at 350 degrees for 10 minutes. Let cool, then place in the refrigerator for a couple of hours. Easy as pie.

4
THE NETTERS

The old man was thin and gaunt with deep wrinkles in the back of his neck. The brown blotches of the benevolent skin cancer the sun brings from the reflection on the tropic seas were on his cheeks. The blotches ran well down the sides of his face and his hands had the deep-creased scars from handling heavy fish on the cords. But none of those scars were fresh. They were as old as erosions in a fishless desert. Everything about him was old except his eyes and they were the same color as the sea and were cheerful and undefeated.
—*Ernest Hemingway,* The Old Man and the Sea

Rayford "Sugar Boy" Futch and his brothers wore skin the color of mahogany. Little wonder. They fished in the brutal Florida sun almost every day. If mullet or tarpon were running, there'd be Futches on the water from Turtle Bay to Boca Grande Pass.

Most of the Futch brothers were handsome, except for Dunk, who had big ears and a nose to match. None of them fit the description of big. The Futches were of average height but wiry strong like the farmers of the sea that they were. Picture a young but shorter Abe Lincoln pulling on nets instead of splitting rails.

Pronounced "Shoog" by everyone who knew him, Sugar Boy accentuated his deep-bronze tan by wearing all white, from the cap on his head to his long-sleeve shirt and his pants and canvas boat shoes, all of which made his face appear even darker.

I remember Uncle Sug crouching like a baseball catcher on Whidden's Marina dock, a nonfilter Lucky Strike cigarette seemingly perpetually stuck

Handsome in their World War II uniforms, these four Futches had a knack for telling Futch Facts. My uncles (*left to right*): Hugh "Preacher" Futch, Rayford "Sug for Sugar Boy" Futch, Duane "Rounder" Futch and Rayford Jr., one of the few Futches who didn't have a nickname. Some of the other Futches were nicknamed Porkchop, Dunk, Brick and Muddy. *Courtesy of Freddy Futch family.*

between his fingers, baseball cap tilted up and to the left like Humphrey Bogart's *African Queen* character Charlie Allnut. Sug could have been mistaken for Allnut, except that his brother, my grandfather Dan, looked more like Bogart's stubble-faced Charlie.

Dan wasn't all Allnut. His persona included a swagger akin to fishing guide Harry Morgan in Hemingway's *To Have and Have Not*. He had a silver tongue and was fond of women, and they of him. Dan was especially taken with prostitutes in Havana. "The most beautiful I ever saw."

When Dan Futch guided his boss and future U.S. senator Mike Mansfield of Montana on Mansfield's boat out of Duck Key in the Florida Keys, Mansfield's friend Ernest Hemingway would show up with a machine gun to shoot sharks. Not a sporting way to kill an animal, and Dan Futch didn't like it. Nor did he cotton to the great writer. "Hemingway was erratic. Nice one minute and a son-of-a-bitch the next."

Spending day after day in the sun creased the faces of Futch fishermen, the skin on the backs of their necks forming a crosshatch pattern the color of a dull copper penny. "They were all dark and wrinkled," renowned tarpon guide Freddy Futch said of his father, Sug, and his uncles. "The sun ate them up. Fishing in the sun day in and day out made them dark-skinned. They were strong men and I mean strong physically. Pulling and clearing nets filled with mullet and hand-lining grouper and snapper made them strong. They were fearless and feared no man."

As my cousin Steve Futch put it, "If they hit you, your brother in Georgia could feel it."

Gasparilla Fishery

In his book *Punta Gorda and the Charlotte Harbor Area: A Pictorial History*, my cousin, the late former state representative Vernon Peeples, described the importance of fishing to the region's economy.

Peeples wrote that in the 1870s and '80s, the north end of Gasparilla Island at Peacons Ranch Cove served as home base for a fish ranch run by John R. Peacon of Key West and his two brothers. Employing a thirty-man crew, the brothers caught and shipped salted, dried-in-the-sun mullet and pressed red roe to Cuba.

In a story for the Boca Grande Historical Society titled "The Changing Face of Commercial Fishing in Charlotte Harbor: Triumph of Ice over Salt," Theodore B. "Ted" Van Itallie wrote about a survey conducted in the early 1870s by George Goode for the Smithsonian Institution and the U.S. Commission of Fish and Fisheries. Goode identified four major fish ranches or ranchos in the region: Captiva Ranch, run by Captain Pierce and thirty conchs from Key West; the South Cayo Costa operation of Jose Sega and twenty-six fishermen; Tariva "Captain Pappy" Padilla's rancho near Cayo Costa's north end, with twenty-three Spanish Cubans and one American; and the operation at the north end of Gasparilla Island at Peacons Ranch Cove, where Captain Peacon and his brothers processed 550,000 pounds of mullet at four cents a pound and 44,000 pounds of pressed roe per year at five cents.

For a definitive look at the netters, Robert Edic's *Fisherfolk of Charlotte Harbor, Florida* offers a close-up of life on the water. In addition to the book's exquisite sepia photographs, there are interviews with surviving members of the Padilla and Darna families, who have fished Cayo Costa waters since the 1870s.

The coming of the railroad to Tampa in 1883, then to Punta Gorda in 1886 and finally to Boca Grande in 1907 changed the commercial market.

Tariva "Pappy" Padilla and family on Cayo Costa, circa 1910. *Courtesy of Robert Edic.*

Salted mullet gave way to fish loaded in barrels on iced boxcars and shipped throughout the South and the Eastern Seaboard.

The future had arrived in the form of frozen water. With the coming of icehouses in Punta Gorda, including the Punta Gorda Fish Company (1897), the Chadwick Fish Company (1901) and the West Coast Fish Company, the Peacons were out of business and returned to Key West around 1900.

Punta Gorda fish house owners made fishing more efficient by erecting stilt houses over the water. The simple, one- or two-room wood boxes built on posts or telephone poles served as way stations and dotted Charlotte Harbor in strategic places like Bull and Turtle Bays, Two Pines near Burnt Store Road and south of Useppa Island in Pine Island Sound. Fishermen would drop off fish to be picked up by a runboat headed back to the Punta Gorda fish houses for processing.

In 1909, the Jones Wholesale Fish Company of Tampa leased land from the Charlotte Harbor & Northern Railway on the northern tip of Gasparilla Island and installed a two-story icehouse.

Fishermen at Peacons Cove moved closer to the icehouse one-half mile north. Some pitched tents or put up thatched houses; others built stilt houses over the water or constructed simple houseboats called "lighters." Large wheels or spindles for drying massive cotton nets were built on a beach next to the railroad trestle.

In 1916, at the current site of Boca Grande Club Marina Village, American Agricultural Chemical Company built sixteen cottages for rental to fishermen, the late Punta Gorda historian Lindsey Williams wrote on lindseywilliams.org. The cove and new shotgun homes became the village of Gasparilla. Van Itallie wrote, "Gradually, Gasparilla became a bona fide village with a school, post office and general store owned by the town's leading citizen, Gus Cole."

Between the two world wars, Gasparilla became a busy center, with two icehouses. Across Gasparilla Sound, a larger icehouse was set to become a major player.

In 1947, Gus Cole moved his IGA store from Gasparilla to Placida. The future lay across Gasparilla Sound, because Walter Gault was set to build a large processing plant that would dwarf the one at Gasparilla village. Gault previously operated an icehouse at Gasparilla that he'd bought from the Dixon family.

Like most netters, Gault chose his words carefully. A devout Christian, Gault never cursed, preferring "Thunderation" and "Confound" whenever he was upset. If he'd lived to see the net ban, he may have found solace in a few four-letter words directed at gullible Florida voters. Gasparilla Fishery closed in 1999 as a result of the voter-approved net ban. It fell on Gault's daughter Eunice Albritton to shut down the business her father operated for more than fifty years.

In the early part of the twentieth century, Charlotte Harbor was a cornucopia, and the netters feasted. In 1915, my great-grandfather Cicero Franklin "Frank" Futch settled on a point east of Placida. Futch was already familiar with the harbor fishery after landing on Boca Grande in 1883 in a smack boat with his new wife, Sarah. He worked at Peacons Ranch before starting a netting operation in the tiny hamlet of Charlotte Harbor on the Peace River's north shore across from Punta Gorda.

In 1916, Futch moved his family to Gasparilla village and owned the exclusive rights to "stop net" both the east and west prongs of Coral Creek, where present-day Coral Creek Club is located.

For five decades, Frank Futch and his eight sons—especially Charlie, who everyone called Dunk—helped make Gus Cole and Walter Gault wealthy men by catching millions of pounds of fish. Cole's IGA store allowed fishermen to buy groceries with chits they received from Gault. Mullet fishermen came up with a new meaning for the store's letters: "I Get It All."

Frank Futch turned over the netting operation to his son Dunk, who lived at the foot of the Coral Creek Bridge in Placida. That allowed Dunk to keep an eye on the movement of the fish up the creek. When it was time to "strike" the fish, Futch's crew would stretch entangling nets across Coral Creek beginning at the end of Thunderation Way or Confound Road—so named for Gault's protestations when something went wrong.

Never bashful, Frank Futch claimed the Futches were the best at catching mullet because they'd been netting them for thousands of years. According to Frank's truth, the Futches go back to biblical times when they fished for mullet with Jesus and Saint Peter on the Sea of Galilee. But Frank lamented the actions of his ancient relatives, because they stole Jesus's share and forced Him out of the fishing business. In the end, everything turned out fine, Frank said, because Jesus became a fisher of men.

The Futch work schedule depended on the phases of the moon, which affected the movement of water in and out of Coral Creek. More movement on new and full moons, less on the quarter moons.

The Futches fished Coral Creek for days, taking everything they could sell while clearing the critters they couldn't. My brothers Mark and Danny and I were six, seven and eight years old and worked the last stop-net operation overseen by Dunk Futch in 1960. Soon after, the state outlawed the practice, because it was killing off other species.

After the nets had been stretched across Coral Creek, the men "balled up" thousands of mullet in one end of the stop net so they could scoop them out. To move the fish into the stop, they would slap oars on the water, all the while clearing bigger animals like manatees and dolphins by lowering the nets.

As young boys, it was our responsibility to remove blue crabs clinging to the nets strung across the creek. If we didn't, the crabs would eat the nets covered in fish slime.

We worked in waist-deep, brackish water not far from the first tee at present-day Coral Creek Club, where the initiation fee is in the six figures. Our hands and feet suffered constant attack from pincers, toes bloodied from claw bites and muddy with muck. We didn't like the work, but were more than happy with our payout: the dog we'd been begging for, a mutt covered in ticks and fleas and given to us by one of the fishermen who already had two mutts he'd found in a ditch like he did our new pup. Pierre lived eleven more years until dying from wounds suffered in a raccoon fight.

GUNFIGHT AT WHOREHOUSE POINT

Any time Frank Futch's thirty-man crew caught an exceptional amount of fish, he rewarded them with a bonus: a trip to Whorehouse Point in Punta Gorda, where a madam calling herself "Big Six" would delight all comers with an entourage of escorts. Standing six feet tall, her nickname seemed appropriate.

Big Six called her brothel "Castle Hall," a house of ill repute on West Marion Street at the current location of Mariner's Village in Ponce de Leon Park. Castle Hall's reputation was known by fishermen up and down the coast, and by cowboys from Fort Myers to Arcadia. Clients were required to check their six-shooters at the door.

One eventful Saturday night in 1892, a dozen cowpokes showed up looking for a good time, only to find disappointment. Known as "Crackers" because they herded cattle with the crack of a whip, the cattlemen had finished their drive from Arcadia to the cattle dock in Punta Gorda, then tramped to Castle Hall for some rest and relaxation.

Anger ensued when Big Six turned the cowboys away, telling the frustrated men that Frank Futch had made a big strike of mullet and bought the entire house for the weekend.

There was no room at the inn for the Crackers, who arrived in Punta Gorda after spending hot days working their way through backcountry pine forests. The cowpokes were hell-bent for leather to take some comfort at Castle Hall.

Trigger fingers got itchy when the Crackers received the bad news. Futch refused to share the wealth, which led to gunfire. No one was killed. Several flesh wounds later, however, a Punta Gorda constable intervened without making an arrest. The lawman stopped the firefight when he talked Futch into clearing out Sunday morning so the cowboys could blow off considerable steam.

Here's the juicy part. Big Six's reputation took a hit when she died of dysentery in 1894. Her sudden death surprised everyone, including my great-grandfather Adolphus Scott Burnham, owner of A&S Burnham Groceries in downtown Punta Gorda.

Burnham and the sheriff were asked to witness Big Six's autopsy. By the time they stripped off her clothes, they understood why the muscular woman had been secretive for so many years.

Big Six was a man.

For more than a decade, Big Six, aka Ollie Bracket, was wanted for murder in Georgia. The law couldn't find him, because he was hiding out in Punta Gorda, cross-dressing as a woman and completing the ruse by opening a whorehouse.

For the Futches, the biggest payday of all came decades after the Castle Hall shootout. "Just before World War II, my father, Sug, held the record of 65,000 pounds of mullet caught in seven days," Freddy Futch said in a 1990 *Gasparilla Gazette* interview.

> *He got three cents a pound. In 1947, his brother, Dunk, caught 167,000 pounds at 12 cents a pound, a record never broken. Walter Gault got a third. Dunk got a third and the crew got a third.*
>
> *Walter Gault got rich off the backs of Charlotte Harbor fishermen. Gus and Bert Cole owned the IGA food store next to Gault's fishery. When you sold your fish, Gault didn't hand over money. He paid in fish house tickets that you'd take next door to the IGA and buy your groceries. Gault got it coming and going. He'd loan fishermen the money for nets and then made sure they could never pay off the loan. Like the song says, they owed their soul to the company store.*
>
> *Uncle Dunk lived in the house at the foot of the bridge that goes over Coral Creek in Placida. Walter Gault built him that house so Dunk could watch for the fish going up Coral Creek and he would be ready to strike 'em when the fish were on the move. One of Dunk's crew, Moon Levens, said Dunk's wife, Aunt Clara, used to sit on the porch as lookout. Every time there was a spring tide and the mullet would swim by the house and head up the creek, she knew a payday was on the way and she'd get out the Sears Roebuck catalogue and order something.*

The wealth and variety of seafood in Charlotte Harbor seemed infinite.

Mullet wasn't the only food in abundance in the harbor. Snook, redfish, mangrove snapper, grouper, scallops, clams and oysters proliferated. Still, you better not venture into someone else's fishing space, unless you had permission.

Stop-netting operations with thirty men would go on for days. In the heyday of the 1940s and '50s, Charlotte Harbor and Pine Island Sound mullet fed troops at Fort Benning, Georgia, and Fort Bragg, North Carolina.

With whole families pitching in, there were plenty of mouths to feed. On one of the hard-packed sandy beaches bordering Coral Creek mangroves, one of the older fishermen would roast mullet over a campfire. Feeding dozens was the responsibility of the men who could no longer pull on heavy cords. Uncle John Alderman served as the camp cook for the Futches. His specialty was cathead biscuits, but he sustained the fishermen by roasting mullet over an open fire of buttonwood.

With help from my grandfather Dan, Uncle John would gut and butterfly whole mullet, leaving the scales on, then salt and pepper them. Next, he would take a palmetto frond and remove the fan. He'd split the stem part way so that it forked off. After impaling mullet on the forks, Alderman would stick the stem in the ground so the mullet would hang over the fire. There would be a half dozen roasting at a time, and anyone could walk up and help themselves—as long as you asked Uncle John nicely. Only then would he tell you which ones were ready.

Life was tough. Fishermen ate what they caught or cobbled together. Mullet netter Stanley Darna said, "I was thirteen when I found out 'fish and grits' wasn't one word."

When the men tired of eating fish, they'd shoot curlew, aka Chokoloskee chicken—ibis to scientists and birders. These days, that's a big no-no, because ibis are a protected species. During a birding charter not too many years ago, ladies from the Massachusetts Audubon Society asked their captain, "Which bird do you like the most?" The guide promptly answered, "They all eat good, but I like ibis the best."

Willie Salters ran a fish operation in eastern Charlotte Harbor, the same area later fished by the Jones family of Punta Gorda. The Darnas, Colemans and Padillas worked Cayo Costa; the Futches had Coral Creek. "In those days, people had respect for one another," Freddy Futch said. "If they had too many fish to take, they'd invite us to come in. That's the only time you did go into someone else's territory."

Frank "Frankie" Jones and his brother Johnny Jones of Punta Gorda were the last fishermen to gill-net mullet in Charlotte Harbor. In the 1950s, their father, Ralph, and Ralph's eight brothers migrated from Lake Okeechobee to Charlotte Harbor, because mullet were fetching a handsome price. The desire in Asian markets for red roe mullet was insatiable.

Alligator Creek near the mouth of the Myakka River was the franchise set aside for the Jones family to fish. "It was territorial back then," Frankie said in a 2019 interview. "Our fishing area was from the Peace River down to the mouth of the Myakka, while the Coles and others from Englewood would fish Lemon Bay, Gasparilla Sound, Turtle and Bull Bays."

Everything changed in the late 1950s, when fishermen abandoned heavy cotton nets. Polyethylene line was the future. Better living through chemistry, according to DuPont. Ten-foot-deep plastic mesh nets replaced cotton ones. They were easier to handle and required half as many men.

The future didn't last long. In 1960, the state banned the practice of stop-netting, in which nets were stretched across the mouths of creeks and bayous and caught everything flushed out by falling tides.

Without the ability to stop-net, fishermen came up with a new way to catch fish: entangling gill nets. When fish were balled up in large schools in the harbor, the new, lighter polyethylene rope allowed fishermen to string together nets hundreds of yards long, sometimes a mile in length. However, by 1994, the Florida public opposed catching fish this way and voted to get rid of the practice.

There was plenty of disagreement between the netters, who claimed they were protecting their way of life by releasing unwanted critters, and marine biologists, who charged that gill nets were drowning sea turtles, manatees and dolphins.

Recreational fishermen tossed in their two cents, arguing that snook and redfish populations were being decimated. The charges stretched the truth to a breaking point. Commercial fishermen contended that biologists and recreational fishermen were lying. Netters claimed that commercial fishermen were the most environmentally conscious people on the water.

Outnumbered, the small group of netters was up against a massive public relations campaign that painted the netters as destroyers of the fishery. Gill netting came to an abrupt halt on Election Day 1994, when Florida voters passed a constitutional amendment banning gill nets. It became law on January 1, 1995, in the middle of red roe season.

Frankie Jones and his Punta Gorda gill-net crew included his brother Johnny, Bill Silcox and three or four others. When the net ban passed, so did his family's way of making a living. "Caught 4,000 pounds of mullet, trout, sheepshead and sand brim on our last strike and then it was over," Frankie's brother Johnny Jones said in a 2019 interview for this book.

The net ban took away a lot of good jobs from a lot of good people. I cast-netted for mullet for a while, but I gave it up. I got a ticket from the Florida Marine Patrol for having fish out of a cooler and on the deck of my boat underneath a wet burlap sack. They took me to court and I had to pay a $500 fine. I said to hell with it. Too many headaches.

What's really hurt fishing is the red tide and pollution like we've never seen before. It's wiped out everything from oysters to mullet. I haven't eaten a Turtle Bay oyster in years.

People with enough money to buy a waterfront view never comprehended the problems caused by unbridled growth along Florida's coastline. Most of the damage was caused by ripping out mangroves, the ocean's nursery, and replacing them with seawalls and condominiums.

According to the Florida Department of Environmental Protection (DEP), over the past one hundred years, Tampa Bay lost over 44 percent of its wetland acreage of mangroves and salt marshes. The Charlotte Harbor region, one of the state's least urbanized estuarine areas, also witnessed a decline. The Florida DEP described significant mangrove destruction, blaming Punta Gorda waterfront development for 59 percent of its lost wetlands.

"It's like my daddy used to say, 'When civilization moves in, the wildlife's got to go,'" Johnny Jones said. "Waterfront property is the worst thing man ever invented."

DUMPLIN' WHEELER'S SMOKED MULLET

True Floridians prefer smoked mullet over smoked salmon—or any other smoked fish, for that matter. But it can be difficult to find mullet, smoked or otherwise, unless you're at a seafood festival.

Cast nets are about the only way to catch mullet since the state stopped fishermen from using entangling nets. If you don't know how to throw a cast net, someone down at Whidden's Marina can catch and smoke you some for a fee.

Here's what my cousin Dumplin' Wheeler told me about smoking mullet.

Smoke at least a dozen fish at a time, 'cause you, your family, friends, neighbors and the people on the next block are gonna want some.

Don't scale mullet if you're going to smoke 'em. The scales protect the meat from overcooking and the fat in the skin acts to baste it. In preparin' mullet for smokin', you have to head 'em and gut 'em and butterfly 'em. Once you've done that, all you do is salt and pepper 'em.

Then you smoke 'em all day using oak or orange or grapefruit wood. Buttonwood is the best but you're not supposed to cut it down anymore. Some folks baste their mullet with olive oil during the smoking process. Remember: You're not makin' a fire underneath these fish, instead build your fire off to the side and funnel smoke to the fish. If you have to build a fire underneath the fish, make sure it's barely lit. If it gets too hot, toss some water on it.

This is a slow process. Somebody asked me how long it takes to smoke mullet. I told 'em, "'til they're done."

5

THE OTHER SIDE OF THE TRACKS

A century ago, fisher families clustering in shotgun houses near Boca Grande Bayou came up with a special name for wealthy winter residents on the other side of the railroad tracks: beachfronters.

The tracks ran through the center of town for seventy years and served as a boundary separating those on easy street from the needy on Tarpon Avenue. Fisher families who lived in the shotgun homes along the shell road called it Whitewash Alley because their cottages always needed a whitewash, paint being too expensive.

Despite the physical and economic separation, class lines were often blurred between the haves and have-nots.

The island's seclusion meant that people depended on each other, getting along out of necessity. Beachfronters needed fishing, hunting and birding guides as well as gardeners, cooks and maids.

Island sailmaker Art Favreau liked to say that everyone from fishermen to Pink Elephant owner Delmar Fugate to gardener Blue Brown of Tarpon Pass Estates grazed in the pastures of the rich. With or without, everyone fished together, danced together and ate and drank together at the old Pink Elephant or Temptation or Laff-a-Lott.

The long-gone Kozy Kitchen across the tracks from the train depot on East Railroad Avenue couldn't be beat for breakfast or lunch. When a country-and-western band rode the rails from Arcadia, mullet fishermen and beachfronters kicked up their heels Saturday nights at the Kozy.

The glue that bound both sides of the track had less to do with commerce and more to do with heart. Well-off beachfronters cared for the community. It was part of the honored tradition of noblesse oblige, in which the fortunate take care of those with less.

"It was a mutual admiration society," Freddy Futch told *Pirate Coast Magazine* in March 2006. "Augie Busch owned Budweiser and would have Captain Johnny Downing dock Busch's Rybovich yacht *Miss Budweiser* at the Pink Elephant dock. Busch would walk over to the Pink and buy everyone in the place a drink of their choice—whatever you wanted. He didn't try to push his beer on you."

One beachfronter, Louise du Pont Crowninshield, made an art out of giving back. She decided that island children needed a school, so she built one. "Aunt Louise" took giving to another level when she opened a health clinic in 1947, because the nearest hospital was twenty-five miles away in Venice.

Prior to the clinic, year-round natives kept their illnesses to themselves until winter, when the Gasparilla Inn provided a doctor for the entire town, not just those staying at the inn.

Before the opening of the toll bridge in 1958, a serious injury demanded transportation to the mainland by a pull car on the railroad trestle to Placida, then a run to a Venice or Arcadia hospital. Pregnant fishwives rarely made the trip, instead relying on midwives.

When Louise Crowninshield stepped up, islanders felt like someone cared.

Louise Evelina du Pont Crowninshield still stands out as the islander with the biggest heart and deepest purse.

Frank and Louise Crowninshield at their wedding party in 1900 at the family estate, Winterthur. *Courtesy of Winterthur archives.*

The great-granddaughter of Éleuthère Irénée du Pont, founder of E.I. du Pont de Nemours and Company, Crowninshield could afford the finest things in life. She owned them in spades. Private train cars. Jewels beyond compare. A Delaware palace called Winterthur.

One thing was missing. She never had children, so she adopted a band of Boca Grande kids, putting shoes on their feet and playing Santa Claus at Christmas.

Two accounts describe how Louise and her husband, Francis Boardman "Frank" Crowninshield, found their way to Boca Grande in 1916. Both are true.

Louise Crowninshield's cousin and Gasparilla Inn owner Bayard Sharp told one story in the spring 2003 edition of *Connections*, the journal of the Boca Grande Historical Society. Sharp spoke about Frank Crowninshield's brother Benny and Western writer Zane Grey setting up a fish camp on Gasparilla Island circa 1915.

The next year, the adventuresome Frank and Louise trekked to this side of nowhere to go tarpon fishing with Benny. They fell for Boca Grande, buying one of the cottages formerly built for railroad executives overseeing port construction. Louise convinced her brother Harry du Pont to visit, and he built a cottage on Second Street, now Banyan Street.

A second story explains that Frank Crowninshield was going around Boston shooting off his mouth in support of the Germans during World War I and wanted the Brits to lose. Frank's public backing of the Germans didn't sit well with his father-in-law.

Frank Crowninshield could hold a grudge. He hated the British for nearly destroying his family's shipping business during the War of 1812. The Brits couldn't be trusted then, or ever, as far as Frank was concerned.

Crowninshield wasn't anti-American. His service to country was proof of his allegiance.

As a cavalryman with Troop K in Teddy Roosevelt's Rough Riders, Crowninshield charged up San Juan Hill during the Spanish-American War. But World War I was a far different engagement to him, according to Crowninshield's great-nephew Lincoln Davis Hammond.

Louise's father, Henry Algernon du Pont, a Delaware businessman who was awarded the Congressional Medal of Honor during the Civil War, was not pleased with Frank's outbursts. Henry Algernon found Frank's pro-German sentiments distasteful, as did most of Boston.

Thinking his daughter and her husband needed a change of scenery, Henry Algernon pored over a railway map of the Eastern Seaboard. After a short search, he considered Florida to be far enough away. He ruled out Palm Beach. His friends vacationed there in the winter, and he didn't need Frank riling them up.

Henry Algernon looked due west from Palm Beach to the Gulf Coast. Gasparilla Island stuck out from the mainland and appealed to Henry, because his son-in-law's words wouldn't be as loud coming from a tiny fishing village.

Banned in Boston, Frank and Louise Crowninshields' exile was a stroke of luck for islanders.

"I'd hate to think what Boca Grande would be like without Mrs. Crowninshield," former Crowninshield Community House board president Nina Houghton said in December 2004. "She sold bonds to build the school [opened in 1929, now the Boca Grande Community Center]. When she couldn't sell them all, she bought the rest. She made a land swap so there would be a place to build the school. She shared her swimming pool with everybody."

Aunt Louise was revered for playing Santa Claus. Prior to arriving in Boca Grande each winter, she'd shop at Wanamaker's to make sure every island child had their dream gift.

"She did everything for us, for all the children," the late Isabelle Joiner of Whidden's Marina said. "There were ballet classes. We'd go trick-or-treating at her house, Christmas caroling. She sent Barbara and I to private school in Tampa. It was a big deal when she arrived every winter. The whole town showed up at the train station."

In his memoirs, Louise's cousin Bayard Sharp described his first trip to Boca Grande in 1924 and the welcome reception the village staged. "My parents were waiting for me on the station platform on the island," Sharp wrote. "It was very festive, with bright covers fluttering from card tables set up with refreshments—lemonade and daiquiris, fruit, finger sandwiches, shrimp and fresh oysters on ice."

For any islander, the Crowninshield beachfront estate, Las Olas, was the place to be and be seen swimming in a pool like no other. Las Olas ("The Waves") was built in 1927 on the north side of First Street at 121 Gilchrist Avenue. The estate still features its magnificent twelve-foot-deep swimming pool with changing rooms overlooking the Gulf. Sue Sligar of Gilchrist Interiors is credited with saving the pool and transforming the Crowninshield horse stable where Frank kept his white stallion, Cheyenne, into a home. Sligar also renovated Frank's art studio on the north side of the Las Olas main house.

While Louise preferred hanging out at the pool, Frank favored the great outdoors, reveling in the hunting and fishing possibilities of Charlotte Harbor. He was a crack shot and liked showing off his firearm skills to friends. With Sam Whidden guiding the way, Frank would treat his buddies to the best bird hunting Florida had to offer, including curlew and ducks in Turtle and Bull Bays and quail off-island in the pine forests near Grove City.

Louise du Pont Crowninshield holds court. *Courtesy of Lynne Hendricks Wiehe.*

There was another side to this man for all seasons. Frank took up painting in 1924, becoming an accomplished watercolorist. The Crowninshield estate was his favorite subject. For a glimpse of the past, enjoy eight of Crowninshield's Las Olas paintings hanging in the Boca Grande Health Clinic courtesy of his niece Toddy Hammond.

In 2007, new Las Olas owners Nicholas and Susan B. Noyes initiated a two-year renovation and returned the estate to its original glory, hoping it would become a gathering spot for their extended Chicago family. When they decided California was the place they ought to be, the couple put Las Olas on the market in 2017 for $14.65 million. It sold in January 2018 for $13 million to a buyer who remains anonymous.

During renovation, Nicholas and Susan Noyes were meticulous about keeping intact the original interior of the seven-bedroom, six-bath home. Except for modern conveniences added to the kitchen, the 4,800-square-foot house is almost identical to the Las Olas compound the Crowninshields moved into in 1927.

The south entrance to Las Olas opens to a great room built of pecky cypress. A fireplace is trimmed in a colorful Italian-tile border rising from the Spanish-tile floor. There are hand-carved doors, one of a sailing ship and the other of a street scene, possibly Havana. The master bedroom and the Florida room overlook 145 feet of beach.

In another unique design aspect, the original great room ceiling was constructed like the inverted ribs and stringers of a ship's hull. It's no wonder that Frank helped design it that way. He was the end of a line of great Salem sea captains, most notably Benjamin Williams Crowninshield, secretary of the navy under Presidents James Madison and James Monroe.

A world-class sailor who won the King of Spain Cup, Frank often manned the helm of his eighty-seven-foot Nathanael Herreshoff schooner *Cleopatra's Barge II* as a founding member of the Boca Grande Yacht Club.

In 1928, Crowninshield joined a flotilla in Charlotte Harbor that included Harry Haskell's *Placida*, Julius Fleischmann's *Camargo*, Alfred P. Sloan's *Rene* and J.P. Morgan's 343-foot *Corsair*. It was the only time they ever sailed together. The club still exists for a select group of sailors with the proper pedigree.

Lincoln Davis Hammond inherited the Crowninshield "Corner Cottage" in the late 1950s. The charming wood home at the corner of Gilchrist Avenue and First Street is directly across from Las Olas. Hammond's grandmother was Katharine Crowninshield Davis, Frank Crowninshield's sister. Besides "Benny" (for Benjamin), Frank's other brother was renowned naval architect Bowdoin "Bowdy" Crowninshield.

Before Davis moved to Corner Cottage in the late 1950s, Frank and Louise parked their orange Creamsicle-colored station wagon in its two-car garage. The Crowninshield Buick was easy to spot around town, and not just for its weird color combination. They painted the driver's side door with the words "Las Olas." On the passenger side of the wagon, they inscribed "Eleutherian Mills," the original Du Pont family home in Montchanin, Delaware, and the name of the family's gunpowder plant built in 1802.

"We were neighbors at Peach's Point in Marblehead, Massachusetts," Davis Hammond said in a 2018 interview, "and would have tea and tea cakes with them every afternoon after we fought our way through the Pekingese and poodles.

"Uncle Frank died in 1950 when I was young, twelve or thirteen. I remember him as being interesting but forbidding. He'd be working on a jigsaw puzzle, and you had better not disturb him."

On the other hand, Aunt Louise was much more giving and outgoing than her husband. But she could be stern, Hammond recalls. "A lot of what she did was about doing good. Her maternal instincts seemed to be strong. She was tremendously generous but could be quite commandeering. If she gave you an order, you damn well better do it."

Frank had a generous side and was fond of his fishing and hunting guide, Sam Whidden, loaning Sam money to buy the property where he built Whidden's Marina in 1926.

Louise was unconventional for her time. Frank, whose occupation was listed as "Sportsman" in society's *Blue Book*, liked to hunt and fish. On the other hand, Louise preferred elaborate picnics on Little Gasparilla Island, where she would implore guests to go skinny-dipping for their health.

"She loved going to Little Gasparilla on their motorboat *Casuarina* that was captained by a very colorful man named Tom Ammidon, who owned and lived on a fine old schooner," Davis Hammond said. "All the women would be naked on the south end, and all the men would be naked on the north end. Back then, there was no one around except us, and there were a lot of us around. There were always dinner parties and picnics. A lot of people in the swimming pool."

Louise Crowninshield wasn't the only Du Pont parading around in the raw. Her brother Harry would walk the beach in his birthday suit when desperate times called for desperate measures. The Du Pont family had a passion for shelling, and Harry went to any length to find a specimen he was targeting.

Bayard Sharp loved telling this story. "Cousin Harry, who was extremely competitive, was walking down the beach, aiming for a spot where a lot of very nice unbroken shells had washed up. He saw two ladies coming from the other direction and pretended he didn't see them and began to take off his clothes. Naturally, the ladies, being ladies, turned around and walked hastily away. He continued his search."

Other Du Pont descendants owned cottages on Whiskey Row, a group of homes north of Las Olas on Third Street. Former professional golfer and Bayard Sharp's goddaughter, Elizabeth H. "Sunny" Fleitas, said Gasparilla Island life was an open book in the 1950s. Her mother, Elizabeth Haskell Fleitas, owned a Whiskey Row home.

"It was free living when we wintered in Boca Grande. There weren't any rules. How you dressed or looked. No one was rude," Fleitas said in a 2019 interview. "We'd skinny-dip at the Crowninshield pool, and because Aunt Louise was plump, she'd bob up and down."

Maggie Lidz at the Winterthur Museum on the grounds of the Du Pont family estate, Winterthur, in Delaware described Louise's demeanor as "quirky." "She wore outrageous clothes and her behavior could be equally outrageous," Lidz told *Pirate Coast*. "Louise tended to be more fun than the rest of the family. She was a hugely generous person and really loved people." Sometimes to a fault. One Crowninshield story indicates the lengths to which Louise went when someone needed help. In a moment of clarity, her Boca Grande cook was trying to escape a physically abusive relationship. After the cook confided to Louise, "I shot my husband," Louise gave her money for the next train out of town.

In 1939, Margaret Fugate, whose husband, Delmar, built the Pink Elephant in 1947, started teaching English and Spanish at Boca Grande

School. To her, Louise Crowninshield was someone every islander counted on. "She was our fairy godmother. Before the school year started, she would invite all the teachers to her house for tea and find out about them. She would come to school and look around the classroom for children she didn't know. She would ask us, 'Who are the parents of that child?' Then she would go to their home to meet them. She wanted to know your family."

Sam Whidden's daughter Barbara Chatham served as longtime chairman of the Louise du Pont Crowninshield Community House. To Chatham, giving back was a civic duty she learned from Aunt Louise.

At the renaming of the Community House in Louise's honor, Chatham said, "I believe we'll never know the extent to which Louise Crowninshield touched people's lives. If she did something or gave something, her friends followed, but they never gave any more than she did."

The people of Boca Grande came to love her, and she them. Giving to children was the driving force in her life, according to her niece Ruth Lord. "She never had children, and the story was she didn't want anyone else to have her money, so she gave it to children," Lord said.

When Louise and Frank Crowninshield stepped off their private railroad car in 1949, townsfolk were dressed in their Sunday best to greet them. The sixteen members of Gasparilla's Pirate Band of Boca Grande struck up a marching song while Delmar Fugate made daiquiris on the depot platform.

My great-uncle Nat Futch—who was always up to no good—had been hired to drive the Crowninshields and their luggage to Las Olas. While grabbing two of the Crowninshields' bags, Nat spied five-year-old Dumplin' Wheeler dressed in Dumplin's best and only suit and said, "How you doin' Dumplin'?"

Dumplin' shot back, "Fine. How ya doin' ya old son-of-a-bitch?"

Frank was startled, but Louise laughed so hard there were tears in her eyes. It was Nat's fault. He had been teaching island children to cuss, and Dumplin' was only repeating what he'd learned from Nat.

Aunt Louise told that story until the day she died in 1958. When she passed, the best of Boca Grande left with her.

The late Bayard Sharp followed in his cousin Louise's footsteps. Like Louise, Sharp's gifts keep on giving. The longtime owner of the Gasparilla Inn & Club and the Pink Elephant, Bayard, along with his brother Hugh Sharp, played an instrumental role in saving Gasparilla Island from overdevelopment.

In the early 1970s, the Sharps and their right-hand men, Creighton Sherman and Wyman "Mac" Miller, feared for Gasparilla Island's future.

Dizzying development along Florida's Sun Coast shot panic through the island's elite.

Without Sharp intervention, Boca Grande was destined to look like Marco Island or Longboat Key, with clusters of thirty-story condominiums.

Desirous of some control, the Sharps, Sherman and Miller created an island homeowner group in 1971, the Gasparilla Island Conservation and Improvement Association (GICIA). Once the Sharps organized the GICIA, they made Sherman the executive director, and the heavy lifting started. They spent years lobbying Tallahassee politicians to give islanders protection from high-rises.

Unincorporated Boca Grande was sixty miles away by road in the northwestern corner of Lee County. With the newest rendition of a Florida land boom playing out, county commissioners trained their eyes on Gasparilla Island, where high-rises would translate to a bump in tax revenues.

By the early 1980s, the Lee County–Fort Myers metropolitan area was one of the fastest-growing places in America, and I had a front-row seat as a government reporter for the *Fort Myers News-Press*. Every week Lee County commissioners were approving large condominium developments along the Caloosahatchee River at breakneck speed.

Gasparilla Island was next, and Bayard and Hugh Sharp would have none of it. But without local control, Boca Grande and islanders were at the county's mercy. Something had to be done.

The GICIA and its well-connected members convinced the Florida legislature to pass the Gasparilla Island Conservation District Act of 1980. The act—the only one of its kind—prevents anyone from building higher than thirty-eight feet, which means Boca Grande could never become the next Boca Raton. The courts weakened the act, but it set the tone for what was to come: restricted development in a downtown historic district.

Bayard Sharp followed that feat with one that sealed the island's reputation as a playground. Sharp built Boca Grande's six-and-a-half-mile-long bicycle path, which opened on February 23, 1985, as Florida's first rail trail. It was not just to give islanders a pathway to health that Sharp wished to transform rail to trail.

His beloved, longtime Gasparilla Inn employee Sylvia Leach, was run over on a moonless night while riding her bicycle along the dangerous S-curve on Gulf Boulevard south of Luke Street, and it affected him deeply. Sharp's commitment to a bike path changed the way islanders moved around.

Sharp made a horse trade with Seaboard Coast Line Railroad after phosphate and rail operations at the port ceased in the late 1970s. When

Seaboard ripped out its tracks a couple of years later, Sharp peddled his idea for a bike path in front of Seaboard's development arm, CSX Realty. They jumped at the offer.

Sharp struck a deal giving him control of the railroad bed from the north end of the island to Port Boca Grande. In exchange, CSX received 127 acres of prime real estate that Sharp owned immediately south of the community center. The land became the site for CSX Realty's 313-unit Boca Bay development.

From the get-go, there was a problem with the Sharp-CSX trade. Shortly after the agreement became legally binding, Sharp was blindsided. CSX applied in 1980 to build 3,600 units from south of First Street to the port. Lee County zoning laws allowed the company to do so.

Boca Bay's plans called for thirty units per acre. To reach that number, CSX would have to build taller than the range light across the street from the proposed Boca Bay property.

Sharp's ire reflected his disappointment. The potential development ran counter to his vision for the land he had handed over to CSX. Boca Bay plans would inundate an island of eight hundred with thousands of people living in sky-borne condominiums tall enough to toss shade over Whidden's Marina on the other side of the island.

Betrayed, Sharp fired back with lawyers, who cited the Gasparilla Island Act and its thirty-eight-foot height limit. He joined GICIA director Creighton Sherman to battle CSX at Lee County Commission meetings in Fort Myers, where they tied up the project until a settlement was reached.

After years of haggling, CSX backed off, whittling their Boca Bay plans from 3,600 units to 372, with a final total of 313 homes and condominiums.

In the end, Bayard Sharp saved Boca Grande from overdevelopment, and CSX Realty received a lesson in who was in charge on Gasparilla Island.

Roger and Louise Amory are best known for building the Johann Fust Community Library on Tenth Street and stocking it with books from the Amorys' home library. Johann Fust was the fifteenth-century financier who loaned Johannes Gutenberg eight hundred guilders to build his press, which subsequently printed one of the first versions of the Bible, known as the Gutenberg or Mazarin Bible.

For decades, a page from Amory's edition of the Gutenberg Bible was displayed in a recessed part of a wall at the library entrance, but it has been moved to a safer place and can be viewed on request.

The Amorys brought in the best to create the library. Boston architect Henry Richardson Shepley, who had designed several buildings at Harvard

University, took on the commission and hired Griffin Builders of Boca Grande to construct the library, which opened on New Year's Day 1950.

The entrance is impressive. Limestone steps precede tall side-by-side cypress doors that are copies from a mosque in Istanbul.

On entering, the stacks are to the right of an alcove leading to a lovely garden flush with bougainvillea along the courtyard walls. A nearby loggia features the Henry F. du Pont and George Melissas shell collections.

The Amorys lived in an apartment upstairs, which they rented out to pay the bills when they weren't around.

The original Bermuda roof remains intact following a 2013 library-wide renovation at the hands of late architect Tim Seibert of Seibert Architects. The roof still feeds rainwater to a cistern that supplies the gardens.

For half a century, Pansy Cost served as librarian; her husband, Tommy, served as caretaker. When Tommy wasn't fixing something or pruning the garden, he helped the Amorys with the library boat, *Papyrus*.

Three days a week from 1950 to 1972, Cost guided *Papyrus* and the Amorys to Bokeelia and nearby islands Captiva, Mondongo, Sea Grape, Useppa and Cabbage Key. Louise Amory would blow a horn to let everyone know the library boat was at the dock. Island families returned books they had previously checked out before borrowing others from shelves lining the boat's salon.

In another nod to giving back, the Amorys built the African American community's Shiloh Baptist Church at Port Boca Grande. Today, it's called Amory Memorial Chapel and is part of Gasparilla Island State Park.

The Amorys took a page from the book of giving authored by fellow Bostonian and friend Louise Crowninshield, who built the health clinic and brought in a doctor.

To help defray the clinic's operating costs, the Amorys renovated the San Marco Theatre on Park Avenue and made it the fundraising vehicle.

Built in 1928, the San Marco was in bad shape after a 1944 hurricane sent the tin roof flying. The building stayed that way until 1951, when Roger Amory took over what looked like a knockdown. Following the rebuild, Amory installed a new projector.

Twice a week, most everyone on the island flooded the theater to watch productions like *The Sons of Katie Elder*, *Hush, Hush Sweet Charlotte* or *Robin and the Seven Hoods*. Tickets were twenty-five cents for regular folks, while beachfronters paid twenty-five dollars for a raised box in the back, where they sat thirty inches above the crowd. The balcony was reserved for the Black community.

A shell floor with a wooden walkway down the middle led to theater-style seats. When rain pounded a steady drumbeat on the San Marco's tin roof, the rat-a-tat-tat forced the audience to read the actors' lips.

Betsy Fugate Joiner couldn't wait for Thursday. Neither could the help at beachfront mansions, because it was their one night off. Thursday night at the movies was a big deal, most islanders eating out before the show.

"At the old Pink Elephant, my father, Delmar, had this great buffet of prime rib, stone crabs and shrimp," Joiner recalled. "Everyone ate there on Thursdays. It was always a mad rush to make it to the movie on time."

Even if folks were early or on time, the projector didn't flicker until Aunt Louise plopped down in her private box.

Like everyone else, Louise du Pont Crowninshield paid Murdock a quarter for one of the palm-frond skeeter beaters he'd make. Without one, the scourge of mosquitoes would eat you alive. No one was spared. All islanders, rich or poor, shared in the agony and the ecstasy.

Like my cousin Freddy Futch said, Boca Grande was a mutual admiration society, where everyone was equal. It's just that some were more equal than others.

Elizabeth "Sunny" Fleitas' Stone Crab Mustard Sauce

Sunny Fleitas features stone crab at her holiday table, a nod to her mother, Elizabeth Haskell Fleitas. A family tradition, stone crab claws were regular treats at Christmas or New Year's feasts at her mother's home on Whiskey Row tucked along Third Street on the Gulf.

For her Christmas dinner, Sunny likes to re-create the cold mustard sauce she and her mother used to make. "This is a sauce my mum always did. It's one of the few things she did herself. She also made incredible eggnog. It was so full of booze the egg never went bad."

If you want the perfect stone crab partner, here's how Sunny makes it.

Combine the following:
1 pint Hellmann's mayonnaise
½ jar Maille mustard (no substitutes)
Juice from ½ lime
1 tablespoon onion juice (squeeze through garlic press to get juice)
Dash of cayenne pepper
1 tablespoon Worcestershire sauce
1 tablespoon ketchup for color
½ pint heavy cream, whipped
1 teaspoon paprika

6
TARPON

F ish on!" screams an angler as the guide guns his engine and races
ahead to set the hook.

A one-hundred-pound silver tarpon zizzes eighty-pound test line
from a 3/0 big-game reel. Braided Dacron thread peels out, reel whining
like a siren.

Seconds later, a tarpon breaks the surface, twisting and turning, gills
flaring and rattling, jumping again and again.

The first few seconds following a tarpon's initial violent run pump
adrenaline to an angler fighting one of the great game fish.

The fisherman's eyes bulge, skin glowing from sweat, then a gasp when his
fish breaks the surface, flying ten feet in the air.

The winder grinds on the reel's handle, gaining a foot or two at a time.

The tarpon tires and turns back to the boat, protesting all the way, zigging
and zagging, shaking its head until it gives in and is off the stern.

Until it comes alive.

Shiny as chrome, the tarpon is still "green" and takes off on another run.

The captain yells, "Stop winding. You can't gain line 'til he stops."

Sometimes, a long first run forces the guide to reverse engine and back
down as his angler winds furiously, the fish still taking out line, water crashing
over the stern.

Once the guide catches up to the fish, it's back to basics.

Keep the pressure on. Keep turning the tarpon's head to the boat.

"Pull up, then three turns on the reel as you lower the rod. Pull up, reel
down. Pull up, reel down," the guide preaches.

Over and over.

After a half hour of over and over, the fish is well done, and so is the angler, who earlier claimed he's battled everything living in saltwater. Until tarpon power puts him in his place.

Off the stern at last, the guide grabs the steel leader, carefully wrapping it around a gloved hand.

With a quick snatch, the leader breaks at the hook's eye, releasing the fish to fight another day.

The angler rolls out of his fighting chair. Winded and red-faced, he lies on the deck wondering if he'll make it through the night. Or at least to the Temptation or Pink Elephant Bar to celebrate.

Boca Grande is a tale of two seasons. One for thousands of winter residents, the other for thousands of tarpon arriving in mid-April for an extended summer stay.

There's good reason Boca Grande Pass is known as the tarpon capital of the world. For a few months, the Pass has the greatest concentration of tarpon anywhere.

Each spring, ten-thousand-plus tarpon up to two hundred pounds migrate to a sixty-foot-deep hole 150 yards off the beach at the south end of Gasparilla Island. Another spot, Lighthouse Hole, is ninety feet deep and where the big dogs hang.

Following a two-thousand-mile trip from South America, tarpon spawn fifty miles off Gasparilla Island from April through September; the biggest tarpon are almost always females, fat from carrying up to ten million eggs.

When larvae grow into juvenile tarpon, they move into Charlotte Harbor's mangrove estuaries to mature. Covering 4,885 square miles, the mangrove shoreline offers an endless buffet of baitfish, shrimp and crabs.

After tarpon complete their offshore mating ritual—and if you're lucky enough to be there when it happens—thousands of "chromers" provide one of the nature's marvels as they roll into the Pass at the same time.

As tarpon settle in for summer, they stack top-to-bottom on ledges during outgoing and incoming tides. There they gorge on critters being swept over rocky ledges that drop from forty-two to sixty feet.

The better a guide is at making a crab mimic one that's free-floating, the more fish he will catch.

WOMEN LAND TITLE AS BEST TARPON ANGLERS

When it comes to fighting and landing a tarpon, most Boca Grande fishing guides believe women surpass men in ability. Over a three-decade period from the 1950s through the '70s, three women rose to become the best tarpon catchers.

One guide thinks he knows why. Billy "He Coon" Wheeler owned a reputation as a top island guide. He insisted that his wife, Doris, was one of the best anglers to ever sit in a fighting chair.

His observations over a fifty-year guiding career confirm his theory that women catch more fish than men. "It's because women listen to what a guide tells them. Men don't listen. Men think they know everything. Any woman will confirm what I'm saying."

Three Boca Grande women distinguished themselves as world-class anglers, two of them claiming records likely never to be broken.

In the 1950s and '60s, Elizabeth "Sunny" Fleitas spent every spring at her mother's Gilchrist Avenue beachfront home on Whiskey Row, an area comprising Third Street and Gilchrist Avenue cottages, where drinking and enjoying life was a competitive sport.

Fleitas was lucky enough to be in Boca Grande Pass one day when thousands of tarpon rolled in to feed, and she took advantage.

In twelve hours of fishing on a glorious day in 1960, Captain Jimmy Mobley on the *Yo-Ho* put Fleitas on fish after fish—thirty on the line to her count—finally landing tarpon number sixteen at 10:00 p.m.

No one—and no man—has come close to breaking Fleitas' most-in-a-day record.

By comparison, most anglers are satisfied with catching one or two tarpon in a lifetime. My wife, Sally Stewart, is perfect, her reputation confirmed by two released tarpon in her only two trips.

A world-class athlete still toned and tan, Sunny Fleitas was a champion golfer who at age twenty played in the 1960 U.S. Women's Open as Delaware state amateur winner. Tennis and golf great Althea Gibson was her playing partner at that Open.

Captain Billy Wheeler at the helm of the *Chico* with his wife, top-flight tarpon catcher Doris. *Courtesy State Archives of Florida.*

Fleitas still plays golf at her private club near Jupiter and shoots in the seventies. In earlier days, the pressure to be on top of her game weighed mightily.

Fleitas found relief from the daily grind of hitting hundreds of balls by pulling in tarpon. Boca Grande and fishing were always on her mind.

"Each spring we would fish every day for two weeks with Jimmy Mobley," Fleitas said in a 2018 interview.

> We'd fish from 10 in the morning until 1, then we'd go to Little Shoal and picnic and swim and have a drink off the stern of the Yo-Ho, then go back and fish until after dark.
>
> Fishing for tarpon in the pass was the happiest time of my life. There was no pressure. I could forget about having to play golf perfectly. It was heaven to be out there.
>
> The day I caught 16 was momentous. We went out at 10 in the morning with Jimmy. As we rounded the phosphate dock and as far as I could see, tarpon were coming from offshore and into the Pass. They looked like diamonds on the water.
>
> Once we started, Jimmy made me fight every fish. He refused to put the boat in reverse.

About the time Fleitas collapsed on her bed that night, there was a buzz at the old Pink Elephant Bar about her feat. Friends refused to let Fleitas sleep, dragging her back to the Pink, where the celebration continued late into the night.

Her love affair with tarpon fishing never ended. The exhilaration of the strike keeps Fleitas coming back for more. "When you have a tarpon on the line, there's a stroke and a feel. Turning the tarpon's head and getting him to turn; it's the most exciting part. I'd have my finger on the line and I could tell when the tarpon had ceased struggling."

Islanders Elsie Bracken and Katharine Jennings staked their own formidable claims as world-class tarpon tamers. Bracken moved to Boca Grande because she was unhappy in her marriage to a Sarasota doctor. She hated the endless fundraisers and cocktail parties. She decided to chuck the demands of high society for fishing.

When her husband offered a trip to Europe, she declined. Bracken had other plans. She told her husband, "Give me the money you were going spend on the trip so I can go fish for tarpon in Boca Grande."

When the good doctor caved, Bracken hired Captain Bill Hathcock on the *Nancy Sue*, previously the *Katharine* run by Billy Wheeler.

Elsie Bracken, who caught 236 tarpon in one season, is all smiles after landing this 180-pound tarpon twice her size. *Courtesy of Elsie Bracken.*

Bracken left Sarasota and the good doctor, married Hathcock and took a deep dive into her favorite hobby.

Islanders still talk about one season in particular that separates Bracken from all the rest. From April through June 1972, Bracken landed 236 tarpon, a record unlikely to be eclipsed.

Tanned with taut muscles like a guide, the ninety-pound Bracken often battled tarpon twice her size using thirty-pound test line while others loaded their reels with eighty-pound braided Dacron.

"People talk about my record of 236 fish but I think it's something anyone could do," Bracken said in a 1989 *Gasparilla Gazette* special edition called *First Drift*.

> *It wasn't a competitive thing for me. It was for the pure fun of doing it. Fishing like that day in and day out for months took a lot of effort. You have to love it. And it so happens that I do.*
>
> *Pound for pound, there is no fish more exciting to catch than a tarpon, and I've fished for sailfish, marlin and bonefish. There's no comparison to the fight of a tarpon.*

Thanks to her Standard Oil inheritance, Katharine Jennings could play in the sun. Most of all, she liked playing with fishing guide Captain Billy "He Coon" Wheeler on his twenty-eight-foot open boat, *Katharine*, the pride of the Pass that became Hathcock's *Nancy Sue*.

In 1959, Jennings paid Daniels Brothers of Fort Myers to build the *Katharine* for Wheeler, then chartered Wheeler for sixty days to fish her exclusively. No one else on the boat.

Each sunrise, they'd fish the Pass, her working tarpon while standing up in the stern, the butt of her rod in a fighting belt around her waist so she could lean back and make quick work of her prey.

Between tides, when the fishing slowed, Jennings and Wheeler would sneak off to Pelican Bay to watch white pelicans and roseate spoonbills.

Wheeler was a tough bird. He was shot twice, once at Bar 17 near Punta Gorda and the other by two U.S. Marines he'd beaten up in a bar fight in Jacksonville. But Wheeler was witty, with a wealth of fishing knowledge and the swagger of a powerful man, something unfamiliar in Jennings's rarified world.

Wheeler made his way to Boca Grande in the same fashion as Frank and Louise Crowninshield, only not on a private Pullman. As the Great Depression raged, Wheeler hopped trains from Tennessee to Florida to find a new life at the end of the line.

Early on, he slept on the beach at Port Boca Grande and made a living by using heavy lines to pull three-hundred-pound giant grouper from under the phosphate dock. He paid a train conductor to ice the fish in barrels and send his catch north to Fulton Fish Market.

Catching great numbers of tarpon required skill. But Fleitas, Jennings and Bracken had something in common: They always chartered an island fishing guide.

In 2021, island guides worth their salt were charging $600 for a half-day, three-hour trip. A full day costs $1,000 and includes morning and afternoon sessions for up to six people.

Early tarpon guides didn't charge nearly as much. Of course, in the early days, fishing equipment wasn't techie, like today's titanium alloy reels and carbon-fiber rods.

In the early 1900s, if one person wanted to go fishing, guides charged five dollars for a full day. If a second angler joined, the guide tacked on a dollar.

By the 1920s and '30s, guides were taking home eleven dollars a day if they fished out of Useppa and fifteen dollars a day if the trip originated in Boca Grande.

A tarpon leaps in front of a guide boat, with phosphate ship at anchor waiting to dock. *Photo by Sarah Peach.*

"When my granddaddy Frank Futch first started guiding, they caught tarpon every way imaginable from hand-line to harpoon," tarpon guide Freddy Futch said. "In the late 1800s, they fished Captiva Pass from canoes towed there by a boat called the *Valima*. If they hooked a tarpon, the guide had to row after it. That took a real man to do that."

My granddaddy Dan said that tarpon fishing made for long days but good pay, even better with a little creative accounting. In Dan's day, guides would take the same people fishing every day for months. To make extra money, guides padded their client's bait bill, tacking on an extra fifty dozen baby blue crabs that never existed.

When customers received their bill, they had no idea if they had used fifty or one hundred dozen crabs during the season. No matter. They were too rich and having too much fun to argue about a few dozen crabs.

As another way to save money during the Great Depression, guides figured out a clever deception involving a sock.

Fishing line was expensive and made of linen, which had a tendency to break and force the guide to spend money he didn't have.

Guides made it appear that customers were fishing with a full spool of thread on their reel by tying a sock around the barrel of the reel before winding the new line over the sock. The hoodwinking made it appear as if the guide was using a full spool on each reel—in reality, only half as much.

So, if a tarpon stripped off all the line and only the sock remained, a guide would say, "That fish took me to the sock." To this day, Boca Grande fishing guides still use the saying when a big tarpon peels off a lot of line.

"Back in the 1920s, if you went out tarpon fishing at 4:00 a.m., you stayed all day," Dan Futch said in an interview prior to his death in 1980.

If you went out at night, you stayed all night.

We only used crabs and vom Hofe reels and rods back then. You didn't see nuthin' else. Tarpon fishin' has come a long way. You can catch 'em all day, what with the different kinds of bait and equipment they have now.

It took a lot longer to go fishing back then. But it didn't matter because people weren't in any hurry. And if the weather was bad, you got paid anyway.

At night, most guides and their people would go to the casino that was in an icehouse over the water off the Gasparilla Inn golf course. There was beer and whiskey, and this was during Prohibition, when you weren't supposed to have beer and whiskey.

We did a lot of things back then you weren't supposed to do.

CAPTAIN BILLY WHEELER'S FISH CHOWDER

For fifty years before it was torn down in the late 1970s, the old guide dock across from the Pink Elephant Bar was home port for island captains. A long two-by-twelve-inch plank provided a walkway leading from the sandy shore through overhanging mangroves to the dock.

Suspended from a piling at the entrance to the Pink guide dock was a hand-painted sign that Captain Carrington Coleman put up as a line of demarcation. It read "38th Parallel," a reference to the demilitarized zone separating North and South Korea during that country's civil war in the 1950s.

Like the two Koreas, an unofficial no-man's land separated the guides. The Colemans, Darnas and Padillas moored their boats on the north side; the Wheelers, Downings, Bylaskas and Futches were on the south side.

The two sides were always warring. The invisible no-go zone acted as a barrier that kept guides from beating up each other. The guides on the north side always seemed to be mad at the Futches. Even the Futches were mad at the Futches.

The north side stayed mad at the south side, because my uncle Lonnie Futch wouldn't give the northsiders any charters. Lonnie had the power to make or break a guide, because he was in charge of handing out any charter business from the Gasparilla Inn and the Boca Grande Hotel.

But if Lonnie didn't like you, you didn't get work. "Nothing on Boca Grande was ever equal when it came to fishing," Lonnie's nephew Dumplin' Wheeler said. "You either ran the show or you didn't."

Guide versus guide. Family versus family. Still, everyone had to eat. And if a guide couldn't get home before the next customers arrived, the guide dock offered a hearty meal to all comers, guide or not.

Typically, Billy Wheeler's Fish Chowder would be simmering in a fifty-quart stock pot near the fish-cleaning bench.

Hostilities aside, there was one thing guides agreed on. Billy Wheeler made the best fish chowder. "It's really a New England chowder with a certain amount of love as an ingredient and takes time to do it right," my Uncle Billy told me in 1988 for the *Gasparilla Gazette*.

The secret to a good chowder starts with something most cooks aren't willing to do. After filleting your grouper or snapper, boil the heads and backbones in just enough water to cover them until the meat is white and can be easily picked off. Set aside meat to include later.

Strain the liquid containing the heads and backbones through a colander. Save the stock and throw the junk and bones away.

Take white bacon and fry it in a small pot until rendered.

To a larger pot, add the bacon and the grease and sauté two pounds of diced onions and a small head of diced celery. Sauté the celery first, because it's much harder than the onion. Sauté the onion until clear but not brown.

Cut up two pounds of potatoes into half-inch to one-inch cubes and put them in with the sautéed celery and onions, then cover with the stock.

Cook potatoes until half done, soft on the outside, hard in the middle.

Take six pounds of grouper cut in half-inch to one-inch cubes and add to the pot. Cook the fish for eight minutes on medium heat until simmering. Heat one quart of milk until smoky hot.

After the fish cubes simmer for eight minutes, pour in the hot milk and simmer for two more minutes. Leaving out the milk makes it a fish stew. Add two sticks of butter. When it melts, serve immediately. Don't cook the fish longer than twelve minutes, or you'll end up with mush.

7
BIG MONEY TARPON TOURNAMENTS

Greed and bragging rights threatened to wipe out tarpon when low- and high-stakes tournaments made Boca Grande Pass a killing field; one dead fish could bring $100,000.

Florida made it illegal to take tarpon in 1989. But the death march continued when made-for-TV jigging tournaments started another massacre in the 1990s.

Beginning in the 1930s, Tampa–St. Petersburg and Sarasota tournaments offered trophies, notoriety and cheap prizes for killing tarpon and stringing them up before tossing the dead carcasses overboard.

The Suncoast Tarpon Roundup out of St. Petersburg kicked off in 1934, with anglers targeting Tampa Bay tarpon schooling off Egmont Key. Thirty years later, an invasion of tarpon killers headed south to Boca Grande Pass.

Captain Nat Italiano on his boat *Spook* remembers the carnage when the Tampa–St. Pete–Sarasota tournaments attacked every night. Suncoast Roundup contestants would trailer their boats to Boca Grande, then haul their kill fifty miles for weighing. "Each boat taking four or five fish. Hundreds of fish a week killed," Italiano said. "Freddy Futch complained about them constantly. It was much worse than Jack Harper's Millers tournaments."

Island guides were hot about the indiscriminate killing, even though most were guilty of killing fish for mounts, though not in great numbers like the hundreds of tarpon taken every month by outsiders hoping to win a cheap rod and reel.

One entrepreneur didn't care. Florida native son Jack Harper of Lakeland saw the potential, taking tournaments to a new level by putting up big bucks for the biggest fish.

First, he needed a base of operations, and it started with a lead foot.

In 1975, a handicapped driver backed into the lone gas pump on the street in front of Millers Marina (no apostrophe) and caused a fire that burned Millers to the water line. Captain Wayne Markham saved the *Flo-Jo II* and a couple of yachts by swimming them into the middle of the bayou.

After the place burned down, owner Wyman "Mac" Miller continued to sell fuel, bait, ice and tackle out of a shed. But Miller was ready to sell, and Harper, who'd been watching from the sidelines, jumped at the opportunity.

In 1977, Harper bought Mac Miller's small operation, which Mac Miller named Millers Marina without an apostrophe. It is now called Boca Grande Marina and includes Eagle Grille and Miller's Dockside (with apostrophe, per the new owners).

To help pay the mortgage, Harper dreamed up a marketing scheme that involved killing tarpon and stringing them up at a weigh station next to the marina bait tanks.

Harper offered $1,000 for the biggest tarpon taken in his inaugural Tarpon Tide Tournament in 1977. As each tarpon was brought in to be

Millers Marina in the 1960s. Immediately left of the building is Sam Whidden's boatways, where many island guides pulled out. *Courtesy of Mac and Pat Miller family.*

Old Millers Marina was transformed into Eagle Grille and Miller's Dockside (*right*), while the old fish house (*middle*) was turned into a $2 million home. *Courtesy of Eagle Grille and Miller's Dockside.*

weighed then hung from the rafters, a crowd oohed as Harper called out the weight. The next year, when the old Pink Elephant closed for renovation, Harper bought the stuffed twelve-foot tiger shark that had been hanging over the bar and chained it to the rafters next to the weigh station.

The sight of tarpon dangling next to a shark flashing teeth was a crowd-pleaser, drawing a constant stream of gawkers and anglers who needed dock space, food and liquor, gas and bait. Harper's circus was a booming success.

A former University of Florida Gator football hero and Miami Dolphins running back, Harper made immediate enemies. At first, island guides shunned his tournaments, fearing they would be complicit in killing their golden goose, even though they'd been killing tarpon for decades for mounts. They refused to bite Harper's money bait.

Captain Lonnie Camano was the only island guide who entered the initial Harper tournament because he needed a new engine, and the $1,000 first prize would help buy him one. The event drew nine boats, every one of them off-island guides except for Camano, who heard the snipes coming from other captains.

Camano caught the only fish and won. Everyone was mad, but the seed was planted. Guides started thinking Harper's cash was too good to pass up. He upped his game again by tossing out an even bigger money lure, and by 1981, Millers Tarpon Tide Tournaments had taken off.

Ethics be damned. Island guides boarded the Harper flotilla when the bounty on the biggest reached $20,000 to $30,000 depending on the number of entries.

Four to six times a season, Harper sponsored a kill tournament on Saturdays from 9:00 a.m. to 1:00 p.m. He always started his contest fast and furious with a blast from a twelve-gauge shotgun from his boat *Bad Attitude*.

Guides abandoned the usual practice of getting in line and waiting their turn to drift through a school of tarpon stacked along the ledges of Boca Grande Pass.

With all that cash on the line, forty to sixty captains jockeyed for position minutes before the shotgun start to drift over tarpon hovering in Lighthouse Hole or the big hole in the center of the Pass.

As the countdown approached, vessels from twenty-foot open boats to sixty-foot Rybovich yachts like the *Miss Budweiser* squeezed together, so close that anglers on one boat could hold conversations with anglers on another.

Boats bumped, disagreements to be settled at the dock. On the other hand, resentments lasted for years, sometimes forever. When Captain Raymond Rodriguez Jr. called my brother an asshole after my brother inadvertently bumped his boat during a tournament, there was a fight afterward in the parking lot at the Boca Bay Pass Club. Raymond ended up with a bloody nose, and the two guides never talked again.

Tarpon master angler Elsie Bracken hated Harper's Tarpon Tide Tournaments, where luck rather than know-how was a dominant factor. "Tournaments take all the fun out of fishing," Bracken said. "Too many boats. The guides have all this pressure to catch the big one instead of catching the most fish, which is where the real skill lies."

In response, guides like Freddy Futch and Nat Italiano and their friend Bud Brown of New Port Richey organized tarpon catch-and-release-only family affairs. Two island favorites that continue to please include the BOMO Youth Tournament and the Red Gill Fish House Ladies Day Howl-at-the-Moon Tarpon Tournament out of Whidden's Marina, where the grand prize is bragging rights and a little cash. No dead tarpon. Vainglory only.

But money talks, and guides heard Harper's call.

Anglers with all the bucks in the world and guides with a reputation to uphold sought prestige and a big payday. Harper's Tarpon Tide Tournaments turned into games of one-upmanship.

Old Florida money from Tampa–St. Petersburg, Sarasota and central Florida gambled on their guides' reputations during the Calcutta betting portion held Friday night at a Millers Marina cocktail party. Drinks and high stakes flowed as fast as a falling tide.

Italiano remembers the crazy Calcuttas at Millers Marina on Friday nights before the Saturday tournament. Wild is a mild term to describe the feeding frenzy in Millers' bar. With daring bets, *Marlin Darlin'* owner Bobby Jacobsen and his entourage of lady anglers from Clearwater and Tampa always added spice.

"People would pack into Lighthouse Hole bar, and it was out of control, because there would be forty boats or more entered, everyone betting on each other's boats," Italiano said. "Big hitters from Tampa and Clearwater and Lakeland jacking up the bids, Harper's friend, Dave Minger of Venice, pushing the bidding higher."

For good reason. Harper got half the Calcutta, that went as high as $20,000. "Dan Doyle bought seven boats one night," Italiano said in 2019. "I think everyone loved the spirit of competition and really loved the Calcutta, because it was so much fun and people made new friends."

A couple hundred people would squeeze into Millers' upstairs bar while Harper auctioned off boats. If Harper or someone else outbid you and bought your boat, you could buy the other half back.

With that kind of action, captains were all in. Why not? They were getting their charter fee with a chance to take home 10 to 30 percent of the prize money.

Harper's success spawned the creation of the two-day Boca Grande Club Invitational Tarpon Tournament in 1983. Organizers sold the idea of a late-season tournament in July by pitching how an elite tournament would extend tarpon season.

Prior to the mid-1980s, June marked the end of tarpon season because the Gasparilla Inn closed. There were plenty of tarpon but nowhere to stay.

The Boca Grande Club solved the issue by building plenty of condominiums on the beach, a clubhouse with a restaurant and a bar and a swimming pool. Perfect for a big party.

But it's not a day at the beach that high rollers were after.

Better known as the World's Richest Tarpon Tournament, the Boca Grande Club put up $100,000 for biggest fish. The second-biggest tarpon received $50,000, while the boat releasing the most fish took home a check for $30,000.

At the old Pink Elephant guide dock, Captain Arthur "Bo" Smith stands with a 150-pound tarpon. Smith landed thirteen tarpon in the inaugural World's Richest Tarpon Tournament in 1983 and won $30,000 and a new Chevy truck for most releases. *Courtesy of the Smith family.*

A Calcutta added another $50,000 or more to the first-place money. Second-biggest fish was worth an extra $30,000 from the Calcutta, and third received an additional $20,000.

The day before the inaugural Boca Grande Club tournament, Captain Johns Knight on the guide boat *Knight Brothers* went on a practice run and brought a 238-pound tarpon to the dock to claim the Boca Grande biggest-fish record. The mounted monster is on display in a room on the east side of the community center.

There was another incentive for boat captains. Buddy Foster Chevrolet of Zephyrhills donated a new truck to the guide who caught the most tarpon. Captain Bo Smith took most releases the first year by using only mutton minnows as bait. Tarpon can't resist the silver-dollar-sized bright silver bait. There are more bites, but the tarpon tend to be smaller.

Bo backed off targeting big fish, landing thirteen tarpon to take home $30,000 and a Chevy. "I never put a crab on the hook, only mutton minnows. I needed a new truck."

To their credit, the Boca Grande Club and tournament co-sponsor, the Boca Grande Area Chamber of Commerce, stopped the killing.

To weigh tournament fish, organizers came up with a clever sling contraption suspended between two pontoons. The weigh master would lower a sling, then lead a tarpon in via a line the guide had run underneath its gill plate and out its mouth.

Helpers winched the sling and fish out of the water for a few seconds to record its weight on a digital scale then lowered the sling allowing the fish to swim away.

About the time island guides thought the massacre was over, reality television found Boca Grande. Starting in the 1990s, a made-for-TV fishing contest killed hundreds of large females during a ten-year run. The females were the target, because female tarpon can be double the size of an eighty-five-pound male. Bigger.

While the club was on the cutting edge of saving tournament fish, the TV jig contests threw fuel on a fire that islanders thought they'd snuffed out.

The controversy surrounding the TV tournaments centered on the use of artificial jigs that snag. Tarpon rarely bite a jig. Instead, jigging tends to foul-hook tarpon in the side, gill plate or eyes, causing damage that leads to death. It takes longer to bring in a foul-hooked tarpon, which leads to death from sheer exhaustion.

Years of protest from islanders and captains Frank Davis, Mark Futch and Tom McLaughlin prompted the state to outlaw jigs that maim and kill tarpon. In the same ruling, the Florida Marine Fisheries Commission decided that no one can kill a tarpon unless it's for research.

Nat Italiano enhanced his reputation by winning four Millers contests and the World's Richest Tournament twice, both times with Howard Frankland. He also placed second twice with Dan Doyle Sr. and Dan Jr. Total take: $250,000.

Life-changing money for a guide, but the ego boost was off the charts. "Dan Doyle never cared about the money, because he would give me a third of the winnings, a third to Dan Jr. and a third to Clark Lea. He also paid me my going charter rate. So for Dan, it was all about bragging rights."

Captain Mark Futch put a couple notches in his cap by winning the World's Richest twice, using his share of the money to build his new boat, *Sitarah*. But notoriety had its drawbacks. Suddenly, Harper started the bidding on the *Sitarah* each week at $1,500 until it fetched much more. Futch wised up to Harper bidding on his boat, so Futch changed the name of his fishing team on the entry form each tournament. Harper had no clue it was *Sitarah*. One week, the *Sitarah* team name might be "Jammin' at the Jim Jam," while next time it might be "Pullin' on the Hookah."

Over a twenty-year period, Futch and George Melissas of Clearwater were part of the *Sidewinder* team that won nearly $500,000 in Millers tournaments and the World's Richest.

In the Boca Grande Club tournament, clients paid $8,000 to enter the two-day, 9:00 a.m. to 3:00 p.m. contest and $2,000 to Futch for two days of fishing. The charter fee included Futch spending several days netting mutton minnows on the beach south of the rocks on the inside of the island near the port.

To make sure he was prepared, Futch and his mate would spend another afternoon with a long-handled net dipping half-dollar-sized purple-legged crabs.

Futch won his first Richest in 1995, when he brought a 124-pound fish to the dock and beat Captain Jerry Smith by 2 pounds. Futch and Melissas put $150,000 in the bank.

Futch's second win in 2000 wasn't so tidy.

With a line of black clouds on the horizon, Futch fired a purple-legged crab to the bottom that was bit immediately. After a fifteen-minute fight, he weighed in a ninety-four-pound fish.

Radio chatter and bar talk sent heavy criticism Futch's way. Guides squawked that Futch was guilty of jumping the gun by killing a small fish in the first fifteen minutes of a two-day event.

A seaplane pilot as well as a fishing guide, Futch always paid close attention to the weather. Before going to bed the night before the tourney's first day, he checked the 11:00 p.m. news. He learned that a front with gale-force winds and lightning was expected to push through in the morning.

In a 2018 interview one month before my brother Mark died of sudden cardiac arrest at age sixty-three, he recounted that winning day.

People were laughing at me for taking that fish. I thought. OK. Go ahead and laugh. I was thinking, "a bird in the hand."

The front came through and there was lightning to beat hell, so all the boats went in to Millers Marina to wait it out.

By the time we got back to the Pass, the tarpon had left. For the rest of that day, we drowned bait. Then we drowned bait the second day. When it was over, my fish was the only one caught. That afternoon, I picked up another $150,000 and my second and most gratifying win.

All guides like to think they're the best there is. And these two big wins are validation of that for me. But I prefer something my granddaddy used to say.

I may not be the best tarpon guide, but I'm amongst 'em.

Spanish Fish Boca Grande

Fishermen like to invent new ways to cook fish. Spanish Fish Boca Grande turns Spanish mackerel or kingfish into a gourmet delight, though grouper or snapper are preferred.

2 pounds grouper filets
½ cup olive oil
3 medium onions, diced
6 scallions, chopped
2 stalks celery, diced
2 medium green peppers, diced
1 12-ounce bottle chili sauce
1 4-ounce can mushrooms, drained
2 tablespoons Lea & Perrins Worcestershire sauce
4 dashes Tabasco sauce
1 key lime, juiced

2 tablespoons dark brown sugar
2 bay leaves
1 17-ounce can Le Sueur baby peas
Slices of pimiento for garnish

Preparation and cooking:

Salt and pepper fish filets, place in a greased baking pan and cook 20–30 minutes at 350 degrees or until you see white foam on top of the fish. While fish is baking, heat olive oil in an iron skillet and add onions, scallions, celery and peppers and cook until tender but not brown.

Mix chili sauce, mushrooms, Worcestershire, Tabaso, lime juice, brown sugar and bay leaves in a bowl, pour over ingredients in the skillet, continue to cook until hot.

After baking cycle of fish is complete, pour sauce over fish and bake for another 5 minutes. Remove from oven, pour drained peas over the top, garnish with pimiento.

8

BEFORE AND AFTER THE BRIDGE

ife was a freewheeling affair before a bridge allowed easy access to
Gasparilla Island.
Easygoing was the rule, and the rules were relaxed. Childhoods
were glorious Huck Finn adventures. Insulated from the outside world, the
only way for islanders to get on or off was by boat or train or cruise aboard
the ferry.

Islanders did as they pleased, said Sunny Fleitas, who fell for Boca Grande
on her first train trip across the Gasparilla Sound trestle in the mid-1940s.

Every year, she looked forward to staying with her mother, Elizabeth
Haskell Fleitas, or her grandfather, former Du Pont vice-president Harry
G. Haskell.

Harry Haskell's beachfront home at Third Street and Gilchrist
Avenue and other surrounding cottages are still known as Whiskey Row,
so named for the sunset cocktail parties where a prodigious amount of
booze was served while her mother played golden oldies on the piano,
Fleitas said in a 2019 interview. Her love affair with the island has
never waned.

*When I was little, maybe eight or ten years old, we stayed at Granddaddy's
cottage, and the house smelled like sand and seashells. The best sleeping ever.
But my behavior had to be perfect and my clothes had to be clean. I learned
to ride a bicycle while wearing a pinafore and riding down Gilchrist. But*

when I stayed at Gram Miller's home on Gasparilla Road, things got fun. No more pinafores. She allowed bathing suits on bikes, shorts at dinner, and I didn't have to dress up for parties.

Goddaughter of island scion Bayard Sharp, Sunny spent her career as a fashion designer who made a name for herself as a world-class angler and scratch golfer.

When she needed downtime, Fleitas headed to Boca Grande for silver king tarpon. "The greatest part of early Boca Grande was the relaxed dress code. Going to the Pink Elephant in shorts was part of the fun," Fleitas said. "Hoke and Ernestine would cook delicious fried mullet or grouper and blonde brownies that were over the top. The talk of who caught a big fish went from table to table. Everyone had fun together. No one was rude. The rum ran rampant and people weren't uptight."

For Fleitas, tarpon fishing was the draw. Each season, Fleitas's mother hired Captain Jimmy Mobley on the *Yo-Ho* for two weeks. "The tarpon were so thick back then that you felt you could walk on their backs across the pass."

Before a bridge to the island, a passenger train in the late 1950s pulls into Seaboard Coast Line depot in downtown Boca Grande. *Courtesy of Boca Grande Historical Society.*

Having fun was the rule, because so many rules that applied to the outside world became fuzzy on Gasparilla Island, depending on who was playing deputy sheriff at the moment.

Prior to the bridge, fishing guides like my uncle Duane Futch and Knight Brothers Marina owner Johns Knight Sr. or deputies Gene Bowe or Jake Simcoe would take turns upholding whatever law they perceived had been broken.

If someone ran afoul, there was an alternative to driving the alleged criminal sixty miles to jail in Fort Myers. Instead, lawbreakers were taken to a cell next to the railroad tracks at First Street. The jail was not as accommodating as the apartment above it. The one-room cell had a single window with iron bars but no screen to keep out the scourge of mosquitoes that would come out after sundown and chew on whoever was inside. One night in the Boca Grande holding tank was enough for anyone.

Regardless, Islanders maintained a general disregard for the law in an end-of-the-line town with four hundred year-round residents. Rum-runners were commonplace during Prohibition, while island pot smugglers got rich in the 1970s.

Boca Grande remained a sleepy backwater until two developers made it easy for regular folk to discover island time.

Land speculators Samuel Schuckman and Robert Baynard became bridge builders when they saw Boca Grande's potential. They bought land south of the old Boca Grande Hotel then platted streets like Pilot, Bailey, Gasparilla and Barbarosa and laid out lots for single-family homes.

But Schuckman and Baynard ran into a problem. Few people in the 1960s wanted property on a remote island. "They had an auction because their lots weren't selling," third-generation islander and port pilot Robert Johnson said. "They thought they were going to get rich but ended up selling some lots for $2,400 each."

Twenty years would pass before home values rose to obscene levels. By the mid-1970s, a home on Tarpon Avenue fetched upward of $15,000, an unheard-of price for a fisherman's shack. Nowadays, you'd be lucky to get one in the seven figures.

On May 21, 2018, cnbc.com reporter Shawn M. Carter wrote that Boca Grande holds the title of most expensive place in Florida to live. Carter's story quotes data on median-home values collected by GOBankingRates, Zillow and the U.S. Bureau of Labor Statistics.

Carter said in his report that "while Miami and Palm Beach tout home prices above the national average, the state's most expensive ZIP is actually

Current bird's-eye view of Boca Grande Causeway and Gasparilla Island looking north to south, with Cayo Costa beyond the southern tip. *Courtesy of Bob Melvin and Gasparilla Properties.*

Port pilot Robert Johnson guides a phosphate ship into its berth. *Courtesy of Boca Grande Historical Society.*

33921, part of the village of Boca Grande, where the average home could cost you almost $2 million."

The report says that living the good life on Boca Grande will run you $177,474 a year. That's before gassing up the yacht.

Everything seemed cheaper prior to the toll bridge, which started out charging seventy-five cents per car and ten cents for each passenger. Today, it's five bucks.

Early on in the bridge-planning process, not everyone was on board with the proposed span, according to pilot Robert Johnson, who was born at Port Boca Grande in 1939. His grandfather Iredell Johnson, and Iredell's brother W.H. Johnson, migrated from North Carolina to Boca Grande in 1888 and started the port pilot service.

Robert Johnson enjoys tilting at windmills. An intellectual with salt-and-pepper hair to his shoulders, Johnson is more than glad to discuss philosophy or any other subject, especially island history.

In the early 1950s, bridge backers saw the potential of a concrete link to the outside world. A bridge meant more opportunities and a chance to relieve day-tripping tourists of their money.

In the mid-1950s, the Johnsons were gung ho for a bridge to the island; others thought it might as well be a gangplank.

"My family was pro-bridge because they felt it would bring more prosperity in terms of new blood and economic vitality," Johnson said in a July/August

2004 *Pirate Coast Magazine* story. "The wealthy beachfronters were opposed to it because they didn't want anyone here but themselves. The guides were against it because people would be able to trailer their boats to Boca Grande and, thus, would not hire guides.

"I still like the bridge because I can just drive off when the island gets oppressive. I love the beach, the lighthouses, the flora and fauna of Boca Grande, but I do like to get away."

When the only privately owned toll bridge in Florida opened in July 1958, it was a non-event.

Touted as a boon for Boca, the bridge initially turned into a bust. "Instead of tourists flocking to the island, the people who lived here flocked off," Johnson said. "Longtime islanders were able to live off-island and still come to Boca Grande to work. The island actually lost population when the bridge was built. We almost had an economic depression."

When the bridge opened, the town lost its footing. Things literally went to hell in the 1970s, when a downtown boardinghouse in need of renovation was dubbed Hotel Hell. "The bridge really was the community's death knell," Johnson said. "We were no longer self-contained. The only thing we gained was convenience."

Clyde and Carol Nabers were destined for each other. Both were born in the same Arcadia hospital, she in 1940, he in 1942, and delivered by the

Boca Grande depot in disarray in the 1970s after passenger service stopped and the toll bridge opened in 1958, offering easy on and off. *Courtesy of Boca Grande Historical Society.*

same physician, Dr. Walter Clement, who also delivered their children Mike and Misty, her brother Sam and Clyde's sister Janice.

Clyde Nabers, her husband of fifty-nine years, owned the Chevron service station at Park Avenue and Fourth Street from 1962 until 1999, when it was torn down and re-envisioned as Gasparilla Properties.

Carol has never lived anywhere but Boca Grande. Carol's childhood home was an apartment in the heart of the village above the Park Avenue retail fish store run by her father, the beloved Tommy Parkinson, who died in 1994.

For nearly fifty years, "Fish House Tommy" surgically cleaned fish for beachfronters and restaurants at his Park Avenue fish operation owned by Gasparilla Fishery in Placida. From 1939 to 1989, Tommy also ran the fishery's wholesale business, Boca Grande Fishery, located next to Millers Marina.

While Tommy or his right-hand fishmonger, Bob Edic, surgically filleted grouper and snapper, commercial fishermen unloaded their catch on the waterside of the two-story fishery, where it was hauled out in baskets and stored in an ice room.

But Boca Grande Fishery was more than a place to buy fish. It was a gathering spot where you caught up on the latest coconut telegraph news, like who was having a baby or who caught the two-hundred-pound tarpon headed to Ike Shaw Taxidermy, or maybe who got the best of somebody in a fight on Millers Marina dock.

Tommy Parkinson's gentle, sweet smile always put people at ease. It didn't matter if he was discussing the weather with a Du Pont or a barefoot fisherman, Tommy was interested in what you had to say. As Captain Billy Wheeler put it, "If you couldn't like Tommy Parkinson, you couldn't like anybody."

In the years before the canals were dug across from the fishery to build waterfront homes, Tommy would walk across the street to the original homes of island Black residents, where he would hand out "sacks of can goods from our own pantry to families in need," Carol Nabers said during a 2021 interview. Then she added, "One man told daddy, 'If it wasn't for you, we'd starve to death.'" A couple mullet or a piece of grouper usually lay carefully wrapped on top of the can goods.

Carol's mother, Mary Ellen Parkinson, was regarded as one of the finest island cooks, her grouper chowder and mango upside-down cake labeled "finest kind" by all.

On the other hand, Clyde Naber's "Best Ever Swamp Cabbage" was such a treat, Carol couldn't get enough.

Carol still can't get enough of island history, as long as the stories are based in fact. Carol is a keen observer of what took place on Boca Grande before and after the bridge and recounted how she spent her days with her father.

Daddy bait fished, too, and he would take me down to the beach at Little Dock next to the phosphate dock, and we would pull on a net all day to catch mutton minnows for tarpon guides. Sometimes, we'd go get oysters in Bull Bay, and he'd sell them to the Gasparilla Inn. Then he'd open them up while sitting at the back door to the Inn kitchen. Half the island would show up, and he'd be cracking oysters and talking with everyone. Before the bridge, the island was one big happy family.

Carol earned the honor of valedictorian in May 1958 from Boca Grande School. Two months later, the bridge opened, and Huck Finn left on the next train out of town.

As the 1960s dawned, mom-and-pop stores suffered through going-out-of-business sales. Clyde Nabers put it this way during a 2021 interview: "Before the bridge, business was close knit because you couldn't get off island. As soon as the bridge opened, people went to the mainland to shop because it was more expensive to shop on island."

Carol Nabers knows the specifics. "We lost a lot of necessary businesses. We lost the bank, the dry cleaner, the telegraph service, the telephone office, even the little jail by the tracks was torn down." In a sure sign of island decline, "We lost the school."

Islanders accustomed to hard times seemed unfazed. They'd seen plenty of strife during the Great Depression, recalling how they worked their way out of jams during the 1930s and World War II.

Despite hard times, island families were blessed with a cornucopia of sea life. "Our backyard was our refrigerator," Captain Freddy Futch said. "Grouper, snapper, kingfish and mackerel offshore. Mullet everywhere. Uncle Dan Futch used to say, 'I didn't know mullet wasn't steak until I was 18.' We'd get clams in the Kitchen [at Grouper Hole near Live Oak Key], oysters in Turtle Bay. Scallops were plentiful. We had it all." Including a ferry service for transporting cars, people and dreams.

Jean Anne McConn Adams's grandfather Captain William Sprott started ferry service to Boca Grande around 1930, his flat-sled leaving its Placida base near Gasparilla Fishery then slow-motoring across Gasparilla Sound to the Thirty-Fifth Street landing, where he brought folks to his hotels, the Sprott on Fourth Street and the Palm on Palm Avenue.

In 1938, Sprott launched a car ferry named after his daughter Catherine. Later, Sprott put his last ferry, the *Saugerties*, in the water. It had previously run rivers in Upstate New York. "Before they built the causeway, most people were opposed to the bridge, including my grandfather, who would be out of business," McConn Adams said in 2004 for *Pirate Coast*. "Islanders like Delmar Fugate, who owned the Pink Elephant, thought a bridge to Boca Grande would spoil the island because it would be wide open to tin-can tourists."

As my daddy, Karl "Muddy" Futch, used to say, "We called them tin-canners, because they'd bring cans of food and never buy anything on the island. They'd show up with a five-dollar bill and a clean T-shirt and wouldn't change either one the whole time."

In the decades before the bridge, Gasparilla village at the north end was the first stop. A dozen shotgun homes surrounded a lagoon, with boats lined up side by side along a white-as-snow, crescent-shaped beach. Next to the tracks, giant drying wheels held cotton and linen nets baking in the sun. A general store offered everything a villager needed, while a post office delivered letters and news from the outside.

"Gasparilla village was absolutely gorgeous. It looked like a South Sea Island," McConn Adams said. "Every family had a bunch of kids. There were the Futches, the Joiners, the Underwoods, the Coles, the Lowes. The Gaults in Placida sent their kids to Boca Grande Public School, which is now the Community Center. And the Darnas sent their kids on the school boat from Punta Blanca."

From Gasparilla village, three miles of sand and shell road led to the train depot in downtown Boca Grande. "There was only a dirt road from Gasparilla Village to the Ferry Landing and then to the village of Boca Grande," McConn Adams said. "But it was really two ruts. The bus would get stuck and the kids would be late for school."

Grades first through twelfth were taught at Boca Grande Public School, which opened in 1929. The senior prom was held at the Community House nearby or in the dance hall at Whidden's Marina. The Fighting Tarpons basketball team beat just about everyone they played, regularly winning district championships. The scrappy six-man football team put the fear of God in players on the other side of the ball, winning state championships three years in a row starting in 1938.

Before the bridge, fishing was phenomenal. A typical day with a guide provided the thrill of hooking into a dozen or more tarpon and catching half of them. Despite the vast number of tarpon in the pass and along the beaches, the guide business wasn't all bread and roses. Strangers were cast a wary eye. Anyone out of place drew quick attention and was discouraged from sticking around.

One Lee County sheriff's deputy dispatched from Fort Myers in the early 1970s was posted on island and wanted to be a tarpon guide. He gave up his dream when he found his new boat sunk at the Pink dock, a large hole in the hull from a shotgun blast. A decade would pass before off-island guides were allowed into the brotherhood. Even after being accepted, an out-of-town guide was rarely accepted into the brotherhood.

Homer Addison, who built the Temptation Restaurant and brought water to Boca Grande, wanted a bridge in the worst way. "The bridge suited me just fine," Addison said in a 2003 interview a year before he died at age ninety-nine. "I was in business and it was going to bring more people. The bridge made the island grow a little faster. There weren't many strangers here when you were forced to take the ferry. Unless you were fishing or had business here, you didn't come to the island. The bridge changed the island forever."

Addison lamented the loss of true island life even as his bar and dining business flourished. "[Boca Grande] seems more prosperous now, but we had a lot more fun back then," Addison recalled as he reminisced about outrageous island parties.

Rich and poor alike got together and had a good time. Every night something was going on at the Narrows [the ferry landing at 35th Street]. *There was always a weenie roast and a lot of drinking going on. A lot of drinking.*

It was a sleepy little village, and everyone knew each other. People would come to Boca Grande and let their kids run free. There was no fear of crime. You could leave your camera and fishing tackle on your boat. The guides might go aboard your boat and drink your whiskey, but they'd leave your money alone.

Sarah Helen Pouncey Peach is McConn Adams's cousin and William Sprott's granddaughter. For Peach, a bridgeless island was a happy island. "Everybody took care of each other. Everybody was your mother and father, aunt and uncle," Peach said for the June 2004 *Pirate Coast*. "The wealthy were interested in helping us better ourselves. Our leaders were our teachers, Margaret Fugate and Betty Jo Thompson."

Peach spent a lot of time as a soda jerk at Jerome Fugate's drugstore. Her next job threw her into the world of high society.

Betsy Fugate Joiner (*right*) and Cathy Klettke talk about life before and after the bridge. *Courtesy of Boca Grande Historical Society.*

Working as an elevator operator at the Gasparilla Inn offered Peach a chance to see the rich decked out in tie and tails, furs and diamonds as they made their way to the dining room. After dinner, the men would retire to the exclusive Pelican Room for cigars and brandy and a game of pool.

"It's nice that we have a bridge," Peach said, "but I'll always be partial to the ferry boat ride and the train."

Betsy Fugate Joiner remembers when Boca Grande Public School closed in 1963. It was a reality check, because it meant she had to get up at 5:00 a.m. to catch the 7:00 a.m. school bus for the thirteen-mile ride to Lemon Bay Junior High.

A year later, Joiner was in tenth grade, and Charlotte County started bussing island children twenty-five miles to the new Charlotte High School. "I remember we were all nervous, because we had to go to the big city of Punta Gorda."

Joiner recalls the disorientation, because Punta Gorda was still a cow town with real cowboys who didn't cotton to African Americans. "It was a shock to see how Punta Gorda people treated Black people, because the Black kids on Boca Grande were our friends."

The new experience opened Joiner's eyes. Punta Gorda wasn't a bad experience. Just a new one.

"A bridge meant we could go to South Gate Mall in Sarasota or Edison Mall in Fort Myers. It was a big deal. Before that, going on a big shopping trip meant taking the train one hundred miles to Tampa."

Nothing would ever be the same again.

Clyde Nabers's Best-Ever Swamp Cabbage

Clyde Nabers is a true Floridian with strong ties to Boca Grande and Placida. His mother, Gussie Cole Nabers, was born in 1912 in a stilt house on Cole Island, now Boca Grande North. His father, Clyde, worked at Gasparilla Fishery and served as Placida postmaster.

Nabers has witnessed countless island changes. From 1963 to 1999, he owned the Chevron service station flanked by the train depot and Fugate's drugstore. Over the decades, Nabers or his right-hand man, Bill Hinman, filled up everyone's tank and worked on their cars. Clyde's wife, Carol, could be found at the cash register.

Clyde spent many seasons hunting in the Fakahatchee Strand east of Naples. It's where he learned to cook swamp cabbage. It takes a lot of work to cut down a cabbage palm to its core to get at the "heart." "I learned how to make swamp cabbage from spending a lot of years living in the Everglades."

Captain Nat Italiano of Italiano Insurance Services is a descendant of a longtime Tampa family and has lived on Boca Grande since the mid-1970s. Italiano said he's eaten swamp cabbage all over Florida and claims that Nabers makes the best.

Carol Nabers agrees. "When Clyde cooks it, I can't get enough. It has a crunch to it. It's not mushy like most people make it."

Cooking swamp cabbage is an involved process. The hard part is getting the raw hearts of palm.

There's a legal issue. Swamp cabbage comes from the Florida state tree, the sabal palm. It's protected and illegal to cut down, unless the sabal is on private property.

According to Nabers, about the only place where you can legally buy raw hearts of palm rests with a man who will sometimes sell his crop at the junction of State Road 64 and Highway 17 near Zolfo Springs. Maybe try the Punta Gorda Seafood and Music Festival in February. The Desguin family has served it up for years.

Here's how Clyde does it:

First, trim off the fronds. Then, with axe in hand, chop away at the bark until you expose the center, where the creamy-yellow heart lies. This is where it takes a delicate touch, because you don't want to cut into the heart with the axe. If you do slice into the heart, it will turn brown. Some people use chainsaws for the labor-intensive work, but Nabers says that's a problem, because any oil on the chainsaw will contaminate the heart, leaving it tasting like 30-weight oil.

Remove the heart, wash it, then cover it with water and ice to keep it from browning. After it sits in its ice bath for a little while, take the heart out and, with your hands, break it into pieces. Do not slice with a knife, because the pieces will turn brown.

Take a big pot and add a good amount of salt pork and render it. Add diced onion and sauté. Turn down the heat to just above simmer, add hearts of palm pieces, cover with water barely over the top, then sprinkle in a good amount of Everglades Seasoning. Cook until the swamp cabbage has a crunch.

"Cook it slow and easy and let it create its own juices. Don't add any more water. That's a mistake some people make. I cook it carefully. Make sure you watch your heat so it doesn't churn and boil and turns to mush."

And there's nothing Carol Nabers hates more than mushy swamp cabbage.

Mary Ellen Parkinson's Mango Upside-Down Cake

Might as well have dessert after a heapin' helpin' of swamp cabbage. Carol Nabers' mother, Mary Ellen Parkinson, was born in Charlotte Harbor, a former fishing and pineapple-growing village along the north bank of the Peace River. Her mango upside-down cake is "finest kind."

2 cups ripe mangos, sliced
2 tablespoons lemon juice
1 tablespoon butter
⅓ cup brown sugar
¾ cup sugar
½ cup milk
¼ teaspoon salt
1 teaspoon baking powder
1 egg
¼ cup shortening
1 ¼ cups flour

Pour lemon juice over mangos and let stand 15 minutes. Melt butter in eight-inch cake pan or casserole dish. Add brown sugar and cover with mango slices.

For cake batter, cream shortening by adding sugar and cream. Add beaten egg. Sift dry ingredients and add alternately with milk. Pour over mangos and bake for 50 to 60 minutes at 350 degrees. Let cool a few minutes, turn upside down and serve.

9

GOLDFINGER

Charles Engelhard Jr. spent much of his time in the air, flying around the world in his ninety-passenger jet *Platinum Plover*, striking deals like a real-life Auric Goldfinger.

The "Platinum King" relished power and had the ear of powerful people. But island time was downtime for Engelhard, who preferred walking barefoot on marble floors at his Boca Grande beachfront estate, Pamplemousse.

His regal wife, Jane, was partial to entertaining at its highest level, her dinner parties attended by aristocracy and the common man alike. She had a soft spot for natives with a gift for gab.

Charles Engelhard wasn't as sociable as his wife. But the nerdy genius owned a fascinating life in business, plotting out every move to defeat laws that governments imposed on him.

When he wasn't working, he was at the track watching his Cragwood Stables horses win frequently.

Charles Engelhard was such a dynamic figure on the world stage that Ian Fleming based his novel *Goldfinger* on Engelhard's exploits. While Auric Goldfinger focused on economic collapse, Engelhard wanted to corner the gold market by buying up South African mines.

Charles Engelhard Jr. was the king of precious metals. Prior to digital listings, platinum and gold prices were recorded on the New York Stock Exchange under "Engelhard Metals and Minerals Corporation," a company started by his father, Charles Sr.

Engelhard Jr.'s fortunes originated from thinking outside the box, never seeing a problem he couldn't solve. When he wanted to buy South African

Jane and Charles Engelhard Jr. at their Cragwood, New Jersey estate. He preferred walking barefoot on marble floors at their Boca Grande palace, Pamplemousse. *Courtesy of All Engelhard and Sophie Engelhard Craighead.*

gold and sell it on the world market, he had export issues. South African gold could be mined, bought and sold in South Africa, but it was never allowed to leave the country. Unless.

Engelhard found a loophole. According to South African law in the 1950s, gold could be exported only if it was made into objets d'art or jewelry. If not, the owner had to sell to the South African government at a fraction of what gold was bringing on the world market.

The clever region of Engelhard's brain sparked an idea. He built a factory to cast gold into baubles and religious pieces that lasted long enough to be sent to Europe for smelting, the reconstituted jewelry and religious objects like chalices turned into gold bars for resale on the open market.

Engelhard's story inspired Fleming to write a passage detailing the machinations of the villain Goldfinger, who smuggles a Rolls-Royce Phantom III built with gold body castings then melts the Rolls down in another country for resale.

Engelhard liked his nom de plume and often boosted the myth by wearing Goldfinger T-shirts to cocktail parties, daughter Sophie Engelhard Craighead said.

But that's the fictional Goldfinger. The real-life Goldfinger was not an evil corporate magnate. Indeed, Engelhard Jr. played a significant role in saving the world from air pollution caused by internal combustion engines.

Under Engelhard's direction, his company's research and development arm invented the catalytic converter, instrumental in turning noxious automobile and truck exhausts into water. The primary ingredient for doing so was platinum, and he had plenty of it, having acquired 90 percent of the world's known supply.

Sophie Engelhard Craighead said the relationship between her father and Bond novelist Fleming is mostly myth, though the two men knew each other, Engelhard Craighead said to *Pirate Coast* in April 2005.

"My sisters, my mother and I always laughed at the connection between Goldfinger and my father," Engelhard Craighead said. "My father certainly wasn't mean like Goldfinger. My father was a gentle soul. He had a great sense of humor about being likened to Goldfinger. He loved movies and especially loved the James Bond movies. He would throw parties and wear James Bond 007 T-shirts, because he didn't mind making fun of himself."

In another effort to enhance his 007 persona, Engelhard tried to replicate a stunt made famous in *Live and Let Die*. Engelhard saw Roger Moore as Bond run a speedboat full-throttle in a swamp in a daring chase scene, jumping 110 feet over a grass embankment, clearing Sheriff J.W. Pepper's patrol car and landing back in water to make his escape.

Engelhard wanted to pull off the same trick, so he bought the same boat featured in the film then attempted to jump over a sandbar near Three Sisters. But this wasn't the movies, and the stunt came to a grinding halt. Engelhard didn't have enough speed to clear the bar near Boca Grande Isles and had to be pulled off. The next day, precious-metal prices dropped on the world market.

Engelhard liked kicking back at Pamplemousse, the estate he named for the lone grapefruit tree discovered at the front of the property on Gasparilla Road north of town.

He loved grapefruit as much as his favorite drink, Coca-Cola, and planted more trees but discovered they didn't thrive in beach sand. To solve the problem of growing grapefruit trees near saltwater, Engelhard spared no expense. He ordered Pamplemousse gardeners to carve out a half-acre swath several feet deep near the original tree and line the hole with copper.

Landscapers filled it with rich black soil and planted six pink grapefruit trees to partner with the lone white one.

The sweet-as-an-orange pink grapefruit trees grew so tall that their limbs hung over an eight-foot-tall stucco wall guarding the estate's entrance. For years, the trees were popular targets for fishermen who needed fresh-squeezed juice for adult beverages.

The Engelhard family had a love affair with animals, taking in all manner of dogs, birds and wild critters. Take for example the raccoon wandering the Engelhards' New Jersey estate Cragwood, or a lion cub that daughter Sophie found in a Bronx pet shop. Engelhard golden retrievers were three-time winners of Best in Show at the Westminster Dog Show.

Sophie Engelhard Craighead added another level of philanthropy to the Engelhard desire to give back. While her husband, Derek Craighead, researches and protects bears at Craighead Berengia South, Sophie focuses on rescuing dogs after starting Lucky's Place, an animal shelter in Star Valley, Wyoming.

Dogs and bears were family favorites, but Engelhard's stable of horses were number one.

His great thoroughbred, Nijinsky, sire of Northern Dancer, was his pride and joy. The winner of five races in 1969 and named Europe's most outstanding horse, Nijinsky won the English Triple Crown in 1970, a feat not matched since.

Between 1966 and 1969, Engelhard bought one-third of the top-quality U.S. yearlings. No one at auction could match his spending. Engelhard acquired so many horses that family and friends held naming parties. As one Jockey Club member said, "He plays the horses the way I play solitaire."

Jane Engelhard was a picture of grace, intelligence and culture. Born in China, raised in Paris and a doyenne of New York City high society, she was partial to Boca Grande because it was where her husband could let his hair down. While Charles liked the cool feeling of marble on bare feet, Jane was all business.

"My mother and father were quite a team, but my mother ruled the roost," Engelhard Craighead said. "He was bright but shy. She charted a course for my father. She was savvy and worldly and knew who to steer him toward or away from. She also knew enough to let him go off on his fishing trips.

"She was brilliant and sociable. My mother was almost like royalty." So much so that in society's upper echelons, Jane Engelhard was given the nickname the "Queen of New York City."

"She was always more formal than dad," Engelhard Craighead said. "Everything she did, she did exquisitely and to perfection. The house was always perfect. She dressed unbelievably. Her nails were perfect. Her hair was perfect, even at Pamplemousse."

In 1972, Jane Engelhard was named to the International Best Dressed List Hall of Fame. The next year, daughter Annette Engelhard de la Renta, wife of fashion designer Oscar de la Renta, was named to the Best Dressed list.

Jane Engelhard's expertise in style found its way to the White House, where she used her artistic instincts on America's First Home, helping Jaqueline Kennedy renovate the people's house. As a member of the Fine Arts Committee of the White House, she was credited with restoring and decorating the Small State Dining Room. President Lyndon Johnson thanked her with a seat on the board of the Library of Congress Trust. She also landed on the boards of the Metropolitan Museum of Art and the Morgan Library.

Like many islanders, Jane Engelhard was fond of the little church that could. The medieval triptych she donated to Our Lady of Mercy Catholic Church was not her first foray into the art world.

In the early days of World War II, she put herself in danger by smuggling priceless paintings out of Paris. Instead of finding a new home in Hitler's Eagle's Nest mountain retreat, the artworks were whisked off to America.

With the Nazis hot on her trail, Jane escaped to New York City. After Charles's death in 1971, she expanded her art collection, obtaining several paintings by impressionist Claude Monet and the original Louisiana Purchase presidential proclamation.

On Boca Grande, her lavish parties were a highlight of the winter social season. "It was my mother who relished knowing people of notoriety and inviting them to dinner," Engelhard Craighead said. "She would have these incredible dinner parties and always insisted there be an equal number of men and women. She brought in the Duke and Duchess of Windsor. There would be current presidents or former presidents. Lady Bird Johnson loved Pamplemousse. Senator Hubert Humphrey and Senator Mike Mansfield spent time there."

Jane Engelhard surrounded herself with interesting people. At the same time, she was equally interested in what was on the minds of islanders.

She required her dinner guests to be able to talk about any number of subjects. It wasn't unusual for her to invite a dozen people to break bread. The guest list might include Our Lady of Mercy pastor Reverend Jerome Carosella, his place card next to me, a fishing guide, who was asking

Katharine Hepburn about her favorite role—in *The Philadelphia Story*—and leading men: "There's only one. Spencer Tracy."

As *Gasparilla Gazette* editor, I bumped up against the rich and powerful. In turn, they wanted to know everything about the island. Conversations extended to engaging Bishop John Joseph Nevins of the Diocese of Venice, Florida, or Brooke Astor, descendant of furrier John Jacob Astor.

As cocktails flowed freely at Pamplemousse prior to dinner, lively getting-to-know-you discussions took place between paired-off guests during two fifteen-minute sessions in the living room, where silk-upholstered chairs were placed discreetly out of hearing distance from the other couples.

When a bell was rung, Engelhard walked the room and signaled guests to change partners for another fifteen-minute session before sitting down to Chef John Nicolas's stone crab au gratin.

At the time of my second appearance at an Engelhard dinner, in 1989, I was thirty-six years old. After a fifteen-minute heart-to-heart talk, I bid Brooke Astor, then eighty-seven years old, "adieu and pleasant journeys."

As Jane Engelhard advanced to where we were sitting, Astor looked up at the statuesque Engelhard and said, "I'd like to talk to this young man a little longer, Jane. Leave him with me." Astor was in the middle of inviting me to go to New York City as her "chaperone."

Engelhard looked down and said, "Be careful, Mr. Futch. She likes younger men. Humor her." I did throughout dinner but declined her invitation to fly to Manhattan, all expenses paid, of course. Instead, I drove to Alaska in my 1984 Toyota long-bed truck to work as a political writer for the *Anchorage Times*, where I reported on the legislature and offices of governors Steve Cowper and Wally Hickel.

Former Missouri congressman James Symington always looked forward to an Engelhard invitation. "We thought we had died and gone to heaven when we went to Pamplemousse," Symington said in a May 2005 *Pirate Coast* story about Jane Engelhard. "We were pampered to beat hell," Symington said. "They had a great Jacuzzi and a great swimming pool. A dinner party at the Engelhards was quite an event. The most interesting people showed up. Katharine Hepburn was there one night, and we were fawning over her like schoolboys. Jane Engelhard was in the upper echelon: great fortune, great civic leader, great looking."

Charles Engelhard died of a heart attack at his beloved Pamplemousse in 1971 at age fifty-four. Former president Lyndon Johnson served as honorary pallbearer. Other attendees included Engelhard's close friends, U.S. senators Hubert Humphrey, Ted Kennedy, Mike Mansfield and Harrison Williams Jr.

Jane Engelhard passed on Nantucket from pneumonia in 2004 at eighty-six.

Sophie Engelhard Craighead once asked her mother why she never dated again after her beloved husband died. "Because there will never be another Charlie."

Stone Crab Au Gratin from Pamplemousse Chef John Nicolas

A cold stone crab claw dipped in a tangy Maille Dijon mustard sauce may be one of the best ways to eat stone crab, but Chef John Nicolas's recipe is in the running. If pompano is the fish of kings, stone crab au gratin is its regal equivalent, having been served to British royalty at Pamplemousse. This is not an easy recipe, but it shows the lengths to which Jane Engelhard and Chef Nicolas would go to please Pamplemousse guests.

Ingredients
2 pounds stone crab claws
1 stone crab claw per serving for garnish
2 ounces butter
2 ounces chopped shallots
1 cup dry white wine
2 cups cream sauce
½ cup hollandaise
½ teaspoon salt
¼ teaspoon white pepper
6 fleurons of crescent-shaped puff pastry. Toast points will suffice

Preparation:

Crack 2 pounds of crab claws and remove meat. Sauté shallots in butter over low heat. Add flaked crab meat and/or chunks of crab and deglaze with wine. Combine a half-cup of cream sauce with a half-cup of hollandaise and set aside for later use.

Stir remaining 1½ cups cream sauce into deglazed crab and shallots. Season with salt and pepper. Transfer crab, shallot and cream mixture equally into separate serving dishes. Cover with hollandaise/cream sauce mixture that you set aside earlier.

Glaze under a broiler, using a watchful eye not to burn. Remove from broiler and garnish each with a warm crab claw and fleurons or toast points.

Serves 6 light eaters or 3 hearty appetites.

Cream Sauce
1 tablespoon butter
1 tablespoon flour
1 cup milk
½ teaspoon salt
¼ teaspoon white pepper

Melt butter in saucepan on medium-low heat. Stir in flour to make a roux. Add the milk until the sauce is thick and smooth. Season with salt and pepper.

Hollandaise
4 egg yolks
1 ½ tablespoons cold water
Pinch of cayenne pepper
Pinch of salt
10 ounces clarified butter
1 tablespoon lemon juice

Put on an oven mitt to hold stainless-steel bowl. Whip egg yolks and water in a stainless steel bowl over boiling water. *DO NOT* let the bowl touch the water, or you get scrambled eggs.

Progressive heating is the best way to make hollandaise.
Whip the yolks until they have a creamy consistency, add seasoning and remove from heat. Slowly poor warm butter into yolks, whipping continuously until blended. Add lemon juice and whip just before pouring on crab concoction and glazing under broiler.

10

GASPARILLA INN

The grande dame of Boca Grande is a reminder of an era nearly forgotten.

More than a hotel, the 110-year-old Gasparilla Inn & Club is a time machine allowing for a glimpse at what came before, a magnificent lady in the style of Queen Anne architecture, her white columns and double screen doors welcoming all comers to reminisce.

Former Indy Car racer Sam Posey was fond of the lady. His first stay was for medical reasons at age four in 1948. Posey suffered from pneumonia, and doctors recommended a cure at the end of a long train ride.

"It was probably the best time of my life," the *ABC's Wide World of Sports* auto-racing commentator said in an April 2006 *Pirate Coast* story. "Boca Grande is a state of mind. I always loved the heat and sun and loved staying at the Gasparilla Inn. I remember when we had to leave. I would be standing on the back of the train as it left the depot. It was the world I loved and I was leaving it behind."

The island was always on Posey's mind. He returned to the inn year after year until he and his wife, Ellen, built a home on the beach with the help of Knight Brothers boatyard carpenters. To Posey's delight, there were only subtle changes to the inn as the decades rolled by.

For Posey the child, riding the rails from New York City on the Palmland Express transcended reality during the two-day trip. "The otherworldly experience started in El Jobean when we were coming across the trestle and could see the water beneath. The rails weren't welded, and the train went

The southern exposure of the Gasparilla Inn in 1919. *Courtesy of the Gasparilla Inn and Club.*

slowly, clickety-clack, clickety-clack. When you could see water on both sides of the train, you knew you were almost there. It was like flying across the water. Then there would be this tunnel of greenery once we got to the island, because the mangroves would press right up against the train."

There was a sense of isolation. Then the Gasparilla Inn rose in the east as the train pulled into the depot. "I remember it being cool inside the inn all the time. And I remember the wood inside and out. And the Pelican Room. Can you imagine building something like that now? A room dedicated as a men-only, cigar-smoke-filled haunt where billiards are played and tarpon conquests are told over and over again."

As far as male-only, it's one of the misconceptions about the Pelican Club. Established in 1914 as a coed private fishing club, members believed "all are equal under fish." The private, well-heeled group included mostly men while giving equal consideration to women with their own fishing exploits. Scandalous reports emerged of women lighting up celebratory stogies, tossing back whiskey and regaling their male counterparts with their own angling prowess.

But there was no place for anglers to gather until land baron Barron Collier bought into Boca Grande. Collier, who owned Useppa Island at the time, paid $150,000 in 1930 for the Gasparilla Inn. Two years later, he built an addition on the northeast side, the Pelican Room.

At initiation ceremonies, members were handed their own key. Now in storage, hundreds of century-old tarpon scales once covered the wood interior like wallpaper, each one including the weights of tarpon landed, the date caught and the name of the catcher.

A world of delights can be found at the inn, with 142 luxurious rooms in the main building and fourteen cottages nearby. For even larger groups, there are five houses and five villas, with new ones on the way north of the beach club tennis courts. At current prices, a night's stay will set you back anywhere from $295 to $2,600.

The front doors open to the registration desk, but the southside entrance is where memories come alive. Twin screen doors open to a porch then a long hall filled with low-slung coffee tables, their tops covered in tarpon scales pressed in place by glass. Each table is surrounded by nap-inducing plush chairs. On the east side is BZ's bar with its purple-and-orange motif—the same colors of former owner Bayard Sharp's thoroughbred racehorse silks. Friends called Sharp by his nickname, "BZ."

At the far end of the hall, the dining room re-creates the feeling of Bermuda, with Hunter fans whirring and its colorful chairs and carpeting. The croquet lawn and clubhouse outside the windows beckon for a game.

Moved in the 1990s from its original Gilchrist Avenue site near Fourth Street, the clubhouse was the former Newberry estate caretaker's cottage.

Beyond the croquet lawn, the Gasparilla Golf Club offers a links course redesigned by legendary architect Pete Dye, known for his stadium course, TPC at Sawgrass in Ponte Vedra.

Starting in the 1950s, Sharp's goddaughter, Sunny Fleitas, spent many winters playing the inn course. "Hundreds of times. More."

For Fleitas, the key to playing the inn's course demands hitting the fairways, where a good lie allows for a chance to spin the ball and stop

Boat House and Guide Boats on Bayou with Rustic Bridge in the Distance, Boca Grande, Fla.

Boathouse and guide boats on Boca Grande Bayou, with Japanese Bridge and Inn Clubhouse in the distance. *One-cent postcard created by Wickman's Photo Shop.*

Sunning at the inn beach club in the 1930s. *Courtesy Wickman's Photo Shop.*

it on the tiny greens. "It's still a funny golf course," Fleitas said in 2019. "What I like about the new course the most is that Pete Dye kept the little postage-stamp greens. You know you've hit a good shot when your ball lands and sticks."

Meant to test the best, seventeen of the eighteen holes at the Gasparilla Golf Club (6,811 yards, pro tees; 6,315 yards, men's tees) are on a small spoil island Barron Collier created by dredging Boca Grande Bayou in 1930. Water hazards are everywhere; the shortest holes are the most intriguing.

For example, take the 175-yard, par-3 fifth hole, which requires a well-placed tee shot over the bayou, boats motoring a few feet below in front of the tee box.

For the tanning set, the inn's beach club offers swimming and poolside lunch while serving tennis overlooking the Gulf.

INN INCEPTION

In her senior thesis, "Race, Power and Memory: An Oral History of Gasparilla Island's Black Community," Kaylie Stokes of New College of Florida in Sarasota wrote that Boca Grande officially became a village in 1897, when future Florida governor Albert W. Gilchrist paid $8,500 for 818 acres and filed a plat for "The Town of Boca Grande" in the Lee County Courthouse.

Gilchrist was the first to try to tame the island. He came up short and, in 1907, sold out to Peter Bradley, president of the American Agricultural and Chemical Company (AAC). Robert Fischer's book *Boca Grande—Once a Railroad Town* details the efforts of Bradley,

Bradley recognized the island's development potential and came up with another scheme when he established the Boca Grande Land Company, a division of Charlotte Harbor & Northern Railway, previously the Alafia Manatee & Gulf Coast Railway.

In 1907, Bradley and his senior assistant, James M. Gifford, paid Gilchrist and his partner, John P. Wall, $100,000 for most of the land north of the tall range light, including the platted town and its beaches. Bradley also added L.M. Fouts as a principal in Boca Grande Land Company. Fouts directed the original team that came ashore at the port on November 28, 1905, with sixty laborers, mostly Black men, who laid the first railroad tracks.

Bradley envisioned a grand hotel for potential buyers of beachfront property, a resort more in keeping with the magnificent palaces erected by Henry Plant in Tampa and Henry Flagler in St. Augustine, Palm Beach and Miami.

He opened the twenty-room Hotel Boca Grande in 1911 to house executives overseeing railroad construction from Port Boca Grande to phosphate mines south of Lakeland.

Bradley had bigger plans. To keep up with his rivals Plant and Flagler, Bradley brought in Tampa architect Francis J. Kennard, who expanded Hotel Boca Grande to forty rooms in 1912, sprucing up its frame vernacular style with Queen Anne influences.

Bradley and his assistant, Martin Towle, bought opulent furnishings from Wanamaker's in New York City to appoint the lobby and rooms.

Immediately south of the main building, architect Kennard added a bandstand and a casino for parties and nightly entertainment. Tennis courts and a croquet lawn were laid out nearby. A beach club and bathhouse were built two blocks away on the Gulf.

But the sporting set needed more. Bradley anticipated customer wants and built the nine-hole Gulf Shore Golf Course across Gulf Boulevard, where the tall Boca Grande Entrance Rear Range Light would go up in 1927.

The 105-foot cylindrical tower at Wheeler Street had a previous life. Built in 1881, it served as the Delaware Breakwater Rear Range Light north of Lewes until it was deactivated, disassembled, sent to Miami in 1921 and shipped to Boca Grande for reassembly.

Golf legend Walter Hagen tees off at the nine-hole Gulf Shores Golf Course south of First Street. Fellow golfers Jack Hutchinson (*left*) and Jim Barnes (*by tree*) wait to take on this beach hole. Frank and Louise Crowninshield are sitting on the bench, having walked from their nearby estate, Las Olas. *Courtesy Gasparilla Inn and Club.*

Building a golf course wasn't Bradley's only project. The inn needed lots of water, and cisterns weren't cutting it. To ensure there was plenty, the inn brought water in by train car.

The renovated Hotel Boca Grande opened the 1912–13 winter social season with a new name, the Gasparilla Inn. It became such a hit that Bradley set aside $85,000 in 1915 to double its size.

A glimpse at what it took to build the inn comes from Karl P. Abbott's book *Open for the Season*. Abbott oversaw construction and became the inn's first manager. He writes:

> *Assisting in the birth of a town seemed very exciting, and the directing of expenditure of what was to me a vast amount of money to build a hotel, help's quarters, powerhouse, guide's quarters, boathouse and bathing pavilion on the beach, also on the furniture, equipment and landscaping, gave me a fine sense of responsibility.*
>
> *We built the Gasparilla Inn, with a beautiful lounge and clubroom, dining room and kitchens, and about 90 rooms, each with a private bath. While pumping out the water to build the hotel, we came across portions of an ancient chest, but we found no gold.*

A 1927 sales brochure from the Gasparilla Island Association Inc., a subsidiary of Gasparilla Inn builder Boca Grande Land Company, features black-and-white photographs of Boca Grande. The island is pictured as a tropical paradise with coconut palms lining streets, thanks to Bradley business associate Anthony B. Arnold and Burton Loomis Jr., who planted palms and hibiscus along Gilchrist and Palm Avenues and lined Second Street with banyan trees.

In 1916, Loomis built sixteen houses at the north end for fishermen and named it Gasparilla village. Pictures from the sales brochure also show tarpon fishing from rowboats, hidden lagoons, Boca Grande Pass in the moonlight, the railroad station, the port lighthouse and beachfront castles.

Another sepia image shows the dreaded buccaneer Johnny Gomez, "better known as Panther Key John, a brother-in-law of the pirate Gasparilla and his cabin boy," so states the sales brochure. "John died at the age of 120 years in Panther Key, Florida. This snapshot was taken in 1895 when he was 116-years-old."

Gomez was known as a world-class liar who fleeced tourists by regaling them with pirate tales.

The sales brochure's foreword describes an idyllic Gasparilla Island setting. "The cottage colony at Boca Grande is expanding some each year, but it is still a small village and probably always will be....Boca Grande was not affected by the Florida boom one way or the other. It has had no boom, will have no boom, and does not seek speculative investors."

The brochure offers a caveat for those seeking the allure of a subtropical, seven-mile-long island. "Everyone will not like Boca Grande. It has none of the usual popular appeal...has slowly grown into its present state of being. There has been no forcing, no artificiality....The typical winter life at Boca Grande has been called an adventure in naturalness. The keynote of Boca Grande is simplicity. One does much as one likes."

COLLIER COMES TO THE RESCUE

With the Great Depression raging, a somewhat neglected Gasparilla Inn was no longer a shining jewel in American Agricultural and Chemical's portfolio.

In 1930, cable car advertising magnate and Useppa Island owner Barron G. Collier paid AAC's Boca Grande Corporation—previously Boca Grande Land Company—$150,000 for the inn.

Barron Collier, who owned one million acres of Florida land, and his wife, Juliet, yachting. Collier owned the Gasparilla Inn from 1930 to 1963 and built the original inn golf course. *Courtesy Boca Grande Historical Society.*

In 1945, Boca Grande Corporation sold its remaining land to H.L. Schwartz, a wealthy New York oil distributor, under the name Sunset Realty. Much of that land became the Boca Grande Club and Marina, with 297 condominiums and homes on sixty-five acres. The club, marina and clubhouse with swimming pool, bar and restaurant opened in 1978.

In addition to the Gasparilla Inn, Collier, for whom Collier County is named, added much more to his holdings, accumulating more than one million acres of Southwest Florida.

Prior to Collier's ownership, the Gasparilla Inn sent guests to nine-hole Gulf Shore Golf Course, built on a leased U.S. military reserve south of First Street.

But Collier was in a bind. Italian immigrant Joseph Spadaro, who made a fortune building a dike around Lake Okeechobee, gained control of the golf course and shut it down to build the Boca Grande Hotel in 1929.

It was time for an upgrade. It was imperative for the Gasparilla Inn to offer golf, so Collier created a course from sea bottom. He dredged what would become Boca Grande Bayou, creating a spoil island for sixteen holes, the other two holes situated across the bayou next to the inn. Golfers would need a place to keep their sticks, so Collier loaded a Useppa home onto a barge and floated the new clubhouse to Boca Grande.

In addition to the new course, Collier was determined to restore the Gasparilla Inn to it past magnificence, first by adding the columned façade and the first- and second-floor verandas on the west side.

As the Great Depression deepened, the well-heeled kept the inn afloat, packing the place to capacity even during hard times. The island was a sleepy getaway for those in the *Social Register*. Prominent families who visited each winter included the Crowninshields, Vanderbilts, Wilds, Saltonstalls, Russells, Paynes, Cabots, Frothinghams, Drexels, Biddles, Pauls, Du Ponts, Eastmans, Houghtons and Wanamakers. Others who stayed at the Gasparilla Inn were a who's who of American industry: J.P. Morgan, Harvey Firestone and Henry Ford.

Collier died in 1939, but the family held on to the property until 1961, when the Collier Corporation sold the inn, its cottages and surrounding properties to a group led by Bayard Sharp, who would later buy out the rest of the syndicate.

Over the next forty years, Sharp poured millions into the Gasparilla Inn. He built six new cottages, upgraded the beach club and added a new tennis center and courts nearby. Pete Dye was brought in to make the golf course world-class.

Boca Grande depot in the 1930s. *One-cent postcard created by Wickman's Photo Shop, Boca Grande.*

But Sharp had his eyes trained on the elephant in the room. In 1976, Delmar Fugate decided to part with his beloved Pink Elephant Restaurant and Bar, and Sharp desperately wanted the only missing piece from his downtown property puzzle.

Instead, Fugate sold the Pink to my father, Karl Futch, in December 1975. It was a poke in the eye to Sharp, who thought he had the inside track because of his wealth. My brother Mark and I were made head bartenders.

We needed help, because longtime bartender Forrest Stover was retiring. So we brought in a couple of linebackers, Pat Owens and Billy Kamensky, who had played with us on Clearwater High's 1970–71 undefeated football team. We taught them how to make Pink drinks while knowing they could break up any fight.

Our fight to save the Pink was ill-fated. Two long, hot summers killed us. We saw business drop from $600,000 during two successive winter and tarpon seasons to less than $6,000 during dry times (between July 4 and Christmas). Feast or famine forced the Pink into receivership. Fugate staked claim and sold the Pink to Sharp, who changed everything, tearing the Pink down and replacing it with cedar, brass and glass.

The new Pink marked another sea change on the island, a point of demarcation between past and present. Drink prices doubled, and mullet fishermen got the hint, sending the netters on their merry way. Guides shifted their allegiance to the Temptation Bar as the Lilly Pulitzer and Izod crowd laid claim to the new Pink watering hole.

Now that he was in the Pink, Sharp was the host with the most. It stands to reason. His mother, Isabella du Pont Sharp, taught her son that a gentleman is someone who makes everyone around them more comfortable.

Sharp also liked being a cutup, enjoying his role as family mischief maker, said his goddaughter Sunny Fleitas in a 2019 interview.

"When we stayed at the Inn we were always kidding each other, pulling pranks. It's what we did, and Bayard was always in the middle of these pranks," Fleitas said. "Frolich Weymouth and Bayard let a greased pig go inside the Inn once and they couldn't catch the damn thing. The Inn was a playground to us. We'd short-sheet each other or put frogs or snakes in each other's bed. It was a glorious time at the Inn. And we played a lot of golf, fished almost every day and took a lot of naps. Boca Grande was and still is the nap capital of the world."

In the early 1970s, longtime Gasparilla Inn guests created a stink soon after registering. To their horror, a color television had been added to every room, inviting in a world that guests were trying to leave behind. People threatened to take their business elsewhere unless the abominable things were removed immediately. They weren't, and naptime at the inn would never be the same.

Over a twenty-two-year period, Captain Mark Futch of Boca Grande Seaplane flew hundreds of hours with Gasparilla Inn owner Sharp. At first, Sharp was a client, then they became friends. Futch would fly Sharp to his East Coast home or wherever Sharp's ninety-six-foot yacht, *Galpo*—Sharp's mother's nickname—happened to be moored.

An avid fly-fisherman, Sharp was always prepared. Two flatboats were lashed to *Galpo*'s topside. If *Galpo* was in the Bahamas, Futch flew Sharp and friends like Dr. Hank Wright to *Galpo*, where they'd use the small boats to target bonefish. During downtime, Futch and Sharp often quizzed each other on their favorite subject: American history, specifically the Civil War.

When Sharp died in 2002 at age eighty-nine, my brother was in St. Louis picking up a plane for delivery. After three newspapers called the Sharp family to get their reaction to Sharp's death, they steered reporters to my brother, because "if you want to know anything about Bayard, you need to call Mark Futch."

"Bayard Sharp was a first-class human being without a selfish bone in his body," Futch said in a June 2018 interview. "He was always concerned about the well-being of others. But you did not want to get on his bad side. CSX found out the hard way when they tried to put up almost 4,000 condos south of the community center, and Bayard worked them so hard at county commission meetings, they settled for a little over 300."

Dr. Hank Wright headed the Boca Grande Health Clinic from 1973 to 1999. In his downtime, Wright traveled to exotic locales to fish with his friend. "You could be with him over a prolonged period of time and you wouldn't know if the man had ten cents in his pockets. He never flaunted his money. He did so much for Boca Grande and its people, many things people don't even know about."

When it comes to island time, it's all about keeping yourself in good company and taking long naps at the Gasparilla Inn.

PERFECT PINK ELEPHANT MARTINI

Forrest Stover worked the Pink Elephant bar and its clientele from the mid-1950s to the mid-'70s.

His approach to building the perfect martini was different than most bartenders. For one, he didn't think dry vermouth needed to be part of the alchemy.

Here's what Stover taught Mark and I when we came on board in 1976.

If someone asks for a dry martini, fill a mixing tumbler with ice and top it off with vodka or gin. I've seen bartenders use an eye dropper to add the tiniest bit of dry vermouth. When you get busy, it's not practical. I prefer to "throw" some at the tumbler from a bottle that has a pour spout on it. If some vermouth happens to go in, that's a dry martini. If it doesn't, that's still a dry martini. Stir until tumbler is frosty on the outside. Pour into a chilled martini glass. Add olive, or onion, which makes it a Gibson.

If someone wants a martini extra dry, there's only one way to do it. You start the same way. But this time, instead of "throwing" some vermouth at the tumbler, you pour their martini in a glass then set the bottle of vermouth in front of them with the cap off so they can look at it. If they want it extra, extra dry, leave the cap on the vermouth bottle. Perfect.

11
HOTEL HELL

The night Hell caught fire, islanders were running naked in the streets. Stunned Boca Grande firefighters answered the fire alarm but didn't have far to go to access Hotel Hell, one hundred feet away, next to Barnichol Hardware on East Railroad Avenue.

As volunteers arrived to fight the early-morning blaze, nude tenants were pulling burning mattresses from Billy Kamensky's downstairs apartment. A pregnant Paula Johnson wore nothing as she stomped on bedding.

Firefighters approached Hell owner Mark Wyman, who was wrapped in a towel. They asked Wyman if he really wanted them to put out the inferno coming from the one-room studio on Hell's ground floor.

After all, the run-down wood structure was in dire need of renovation and a paint job. Sixty years of wear and tear on Hotel Hell gave the heart pine building a certain ghetto charm. Hell was saved, but Wyman's insurers considered the place a total loss and gave him $50,000.

"The fire was a godsend for me," Wyman said in 2021. "I had a $50,000 note due, and the insurance from the fire paid off the note."

On that fateful night, as fire ripped through Hell, Boca's first responders didn't wait for Wyman's answer. They saved enough of Hell that night in 1983 for a new owner to rebuild. As a result, downtown Boca Grande would flourish when Lee County used Hotel Hell as a test case to create a new countywide historic preservation district law.

No one's sure who built Hotel Hell in 1917. Fishing guide Mac Mickle owned Mickle Apartments in the 1940s and charged $3.50 per day for a room. Another $15.00, and Mack would take you fishing all day. His wife,

Hotel Hell in the 1980s, through the eyes of watercolorist Patti Middleton. *Courtesy Middleton family.*

Blonnie, operated a beauty shop on the ground floor. In the back, my grandma Nellie washed clothes for the rich and literally laundered and ironed their money so it would be crisp.

The Mickles sold to Ruby and Pete Scott in the late 1960s, and new tenants called it Ruby's Green Apartments because of its color. In 1980, Chicago investor Mark Wyman put down $15,000 and renamed it Hotel Hell. Many islanders considered the place an eyesore, and so did Wyman.

Islander Hank Browne, who bought Hell in the 1990s and turned it into condominiums, believes the Charlotte Harbor & Northern Railway erected the nameless building to house workers. His theory was based on Hell's small rooms and a common cooking area in the rear of the building.

Hotel Hell became Hotel H while serving as the test case for Lee County's historic preservation district rules. *Courtesy Boca Grande Historical Society.*

But Browne didn't save Hell. Architect Rick Thurkow took on Hell's renovation and, in turn, helped rescue downtown Boca Grande from a steady decline.

In 1986, Copper Nail owner-architect Thurkow made Wyman an offer for what was left of Hell and then spent nearly three years and $150,000 restoring the boardinghouse.

Along the way, Hell's renovation became the blueprint for Lee County's historic preservation rules, passed in 1988. By June 1990, Lee County planners created Boca Grande's historic district for 134 properties running from First Street to Twentieth Street except for Waterways Avenue, the Dam streets and the east side of Palm Avenue where it meets Waterways.

Investors took notice. They flocked to the island, targeting downtown buildings such as the train depot, which received a makeover and became home to an ice-cream parlor, dress and gift shops on the first floor and a legal office on the second. In 1999, Clyde Nabers sold his Chevron gas station, the new owners tearing it down to make room for Gasparilla Properties.

In the late 1970s, Ruby and Pete Scott sold Hell to Wyman with one stipulation: He couldn't increase rent on anyone living there. "Ruby Scott was holding paper on the building, and it was written in the contract that I couldn't raise the rent or kick out the old people," Wyman said for a May 2004 *Pirate Coast* story. "They were only paying $100 a month. I found it nothing but hell trying to get rent while trying to keep the building from collapsing. It was hell, and I named it so."

Thurkow the architect renamed it Hotel H. Luxury home general contractor McHugh-Porter now calls it home. Additionally, there are several apartments, though they rent for more than the seventy-five dollars a month I paid when I lived there in 1976.

About the time Wyman rolled in from Chicago in the mid-1970s, some parts of downtown were ailing. Teens with rocks—or anyone with a gun—used the train depot windows for target practice. Or they took vengeance on the long-closed Boca Grande School, now the Community Center, where the warped pine floors in the auditorium sagged following years of neglect.

There was talk of razing Hell. Even the school was under consideration.

Hell's front entrance opened to a screened-in porch and stairwell. No need for air-conditioning in the front apartment on the second floor—the ventilation system was au natural, because there was a hole in the wall big enough to climb through. That three-room studio was my home in 1976, when I was bartending at the old Pink Elephant. No charge for cockroaches so big they feared no one when the lights were switched on.

Despite its drawbacks, Hell was a great place to live. If you squinted hard enough, you could see a sliver of the Gulf from the second-floor porch. Tenants were a close-knit group; they never locked their doors. With holes in the walls, it was pointless.

"Windy City" Wyman did his best to offer amenities, like coin laundry machines charging fifty cents a load. "Open 24 hours. We doze but never close." He never made any money, because tenants robbed the coin box to buy beer.

Donald "Wharf Rat" Casey was the prime suspect in the coin-box thievery. Wharf Rat lived on the second floor in the rear. He was the unofficial mayor of Boca Grande, so named by islanders who frequented the Temptation bar or Millers Marina or the Laff-a-Lott. The sharp-witted Casey was never shy about dispensing his opinions, but he never wished anyone ill will.

"He was a kind drunk," according to Bob Edic, Hotel Hell manager/tenant. "Back in the '70s, everyone took turns being the town drunk. It seemed like Wharf Rat's turn came every other day."

Collecting rent was troublesome for Wyman, even though it was less than $100 a month for each of six apartments, not including the third-floor attic space. Edic struggled to wrestle anything from Gene Sampley, who alternately lived on the second floor or in the attic, depending on the amount of work he did as resident handyman.

"If I got $600 or $700, I didn't have to pay rent that month," Edic said. "If someone didn't pay, they had to move to the porch. Wharf Rat spent a few nights on the porch."

According to Edic, Wharf Rat was responsible for a lot of excitement in Hell. "The fire department showed up one night, smoke billowing out a window. Wharf Rat was barbecuing hamburgers over a wood fire he had built in the kitchen sink."

It wasn't the last time Hell would burn. But it's one of the last times anyone saw Donald Casey. He died in 1993 in a mysterious accident in Salem, Massachusetts. Casey was fifty-two.

Edic's daughter Darlene Edic Crawford said growing up in Hell "was an experience that made me a better person. It gave me a lifestyle completely foreign to most people. It also taught me compassion."

It may have looked like tenement housing, but Crawford, a nurse, said Hotel Hell was the first place she lived where there was a solid roof over her head. Before that, the family eked out an existence while living in a tent on Cole Island. At least Darlene's new home was dry. She had a radio but no television. Then a big surprise came her senior year of high school. Her father installed an air conditioner, which he hung precariously from her bedroom window.

Where is Boca Grande?

———o———

Down on Gasparilla Isle
Where the sun shines all the while;
Where winter's snow was never known to go.
Where the palm leaves keep a-swaying
When the wind's among them playing
And makes the softest music as they blow.

Down where the sun shines a little brighter,
And the sea sands drift a trifle whiter
And happiness is easy to be had.
Where the sky and ocean's bluer
And hearts beat a little truer,
And any little thing just makes you glad.

Down where you make friends a little quicker
Where your blood flows a little thicker,
And dull care simply slips away.
Where the fish will always bite,
Where the weather's always right,
And every day's a happy summer day.

Down where the sun sinks at night
In a soft refulgent light
Of purple, gold and gorgeous red and blue,
And with a golden promise blest
Goes to that Final land of rest
Where some day you and I shall travel too.

J. M.

"Where is Boca Grande?" isn't as much about location as it is about a state of mind and keeping yourself in good company. *Courtesy Boca Grande Historical Society.*

"We lived above Tommy Parkinson's fish house and for a while on Cole Island, but for the longest time we were in Hell. Someone turned the fish house into a multi-million-dollar home, Cole Island is Boca Grande North and Hotel Hell is Hotel H. Does anyone living around here know that?"

There were plenty of sinners on Boca Grande, which made for a crowded house in Hell. "There were people living in every nook and cranny as well as overnight guests who slept on the porch," Crawford said. "The guys who lived upstairs were very nice. Respectful and polite but always seemed to be in a stupor. Once in a while I did have to step over naked bodies in the hallway."

Most of Darlene's friends weren't allowed to do a sleepover. Hell's reputation preceded it. Mostly bad. "There were so many rumors about what went on in Hell," she said, "and most of them were true."

She and her brother Dennis shared a second-floor room over her parents' first-floor apartment. They also shared a bathroom with tenants from two other apartments as well as Sampley in the attic. "The bathroom situation was not good," Crawford said. "I tried to clean it but it was a losing battle. At least there was a sink in my room."

Dennis remembers Hell as "nothing but fun with a lot of funny things going on" and told *Pirate Coast* in 2004 about his favorite story involving Sampley.

> *Gene was the handyman and would trade for rent and there was always a discrepancy about how much work Gene did or didn't do around the place, and he and Mark were always fighting about it.*
>
> *Mark kicked him out and Gene would have none of it, so he moved into the attic because he had no place to go. So Mark thought Gene was out, or at least not around. A couple showed up and rented the apartment where Gene had been living. Nobody including Mark knew Gene had moved into the attic, or what we called the "third-floor" apartment. The new tenants were sitting in the apartment when the drop stairs came out of the ceiling and Gene climbed down. They didn't stick around.*

The big fire almost put an end to Hell, gutting Kamensky's bottom-floor apartment, where it started. The only thing that survived was Kamensky's Jack Barndollar watercolor of a schooner, saved by falling facedown off the wall and onto the floor. The cause of the fire was never discovered, though some blame a candle left burning after an all-night session of whatever went on in Hell.

Tearing down the building seemed the only option, until the cavalry from Lee County rode into town.

Former CIA director and U.S. congressman Porter Goss served as a Lee County commissioner at the time of the fire. He represented Boca Grande when the county decided it was time to test the waters leading to the creation of the county's first historic district. Goss spent a lot of time on Boca Grande trying to get a handle on the mishmash of downtown buildings and homes.

"There are a lot of flavors on Boca Grande," Goss said in a 1983 story in the *Fort Myers News-Press*. "The difficult part is trying to figure out what those flavors are. The whole community is cockeyed when it comes to conforming to existing [zoning] regulations. Nearly every building in the community violates existing regulations. The buildings are too close together. They cover too much of their lots. Property isn't zoned correctly. The list goes on and on."

And Hell became the first convert.

Without Hell and architect Thurkow's perseverance, Boca Grande would look different than it does today.

The only thing Thurkow saved when he took over was the cedar siding. He even changed the name to Hotel H as a concession to Lee County. Despite an awning out front that reads "McHugh-Porter," most native islanders still call it Hotel Hell.

Hank and Suzie Browne bought Hotel H from Thurkow not solely for the investment opportunity but also because they loved old buildings. Hank graduated from the University of Virginia, which put a premium on venerable structures. He spent a good portion of his life in the restoration business. Ironically, Browne was responsible for renovating more than thirty churches, including Pohick Episcopal Church in Fairfax, Virginia, where George Washington prayed.

"I think Hotel Hell is a landmark that's not well known and is a testament to the construction skills of the railroad," Browne said in 2004.

Suzie Browne added that after buying Hell, she wanted to throw a party for everyone who ever lived there. "Then I realized I'd have to throw a party for 1,000 people."

So if you're ever ambling along East Railroad Avenue with nothing to do, you can just go to Hell.

Karl's Pepper Jelly with a Nod to Mabel Oller

My father, Karl "Muddy" Futch, was a fisherman/Florida Highway patrolman/raconteur/banker and restaurant owner. He always said you had to be versatile to survive. Most of all, he enjoyed all things spicy and fiery hot, whether food or life itself.

In his honor, while at the same time honoring Hotel Hell, here's a recipe for Karl's Pepper Jelly refined from a recipe by Mabel Oller.

¼ cup ground jalapeno pepper
¾ cup ground bell pepper
1½ cups cider vinegar
6½ cups sugar
6 ounces fruit pectin

Mix all ingredients and let come to a rolling boil. Remove from heat and let cool 10 minutes. Add fruit pectin and stir well. Immediately put into jelly jars. Cool, seal and serve with meats and casseroles.

12
A TOWN BUILT ON PHOSPHATE

Boca Grande wouldn't be paradise without phosphate. The island's fate can be traced to the white-and-yellow rock mined in central Florida then shipped by rail to Port Boca Grande.

Without phosphate, Gasparilla Island might have become like its uninhabited sister to the south, Cayo Costa.

But the world needed fertilizer to grow food for a population explosion fostered by the Industrial Revolution. Lucky for man and Boca Grande, the world's largest phosphate deposits were discovered sixty miles away in 1881.

While surveying where to dig a canal to connect the Gulf of Mexico to the Atlantic, U.S. Army Corps of Engineers chief engineer Captain J. Francis LeBaron found pebble phosphate along the Peace River in Polk County.

Nobody paid much attention until 1886, when John C. Jones and Captain W.R. McKee stumbled upon high-grade phosphate during a hunting trip. Miles of riverbank revealed exposed phosphate.

But it's Joseph Hull of South Carolina who gets to shout, "Eureka!" Hull bought up inexpensive land south of Arcadia and formed the Peace River Phosphate Mining Company.

Industrialist Peter Bradley took notice, investing in land near Bartow and Lakeland.

A crucial moment in Boca Grande's history hinged on a business deal that Bradley, owner of the Bradley Fertilizer Works in North Weymouth, Massachusetts, put into motion. In 1894, he partnered with Joseph Hull's operation. With the addition of Bradley's land, Hull's Peace River Mining Company holdings grew to 24,000 acres.

Downtown Boca Grande circa 1920, with phosphate train delivering to the port. *Courtesy of Burgett Bros. Photography, Tampa.*

By 1899, Bradley's newly formed American Agricultural Chemical Company had swallowed up Peace River Phosphate Mining Company.

Bradley started shipping phosphate along six miles of railroad to a spot where it was loaded onto barges then floated down the Peace River to Punta Gorda to waiting shallow-draft schooners. To Bradley, barging the phosphate was outdated technology. What he needed was a railroad to a port. He looked to the south end of Gasparilla Island, where the deepest natural pass on the Eastern Seaboard would give him direct access to four- and five-mast schooners plying the Gulf of Mexico.

In January 1905, Bradley's American Agricultural Chemical bought the charter to build a railroad from Port Boca Grande to a point south of Lakeland. On November 25, 1905, the steamboat *Mistletoe* put ashore on the Gulf side beach near the port lighthouse.

Engineer L.M. Fouts and sixty laborers pitched tents in the shadow of the lighthouse. Mosquitoes were plentiful, supplies limited. A lot of beans and local fish. Hoecake was the only fresh bread available.

Bradley named AAC's transport arm the Charlotte Harbor & Northern Railway (CH&N). Poor fisher families made up their own name, because not many natives made any money off the railroad. Because life was so hard on Gasparilla Island, islanders took the first three letters and dubbed the railway the "Cold, Hungry and Naked."

The port opened in 1910, and the days of loading phosphate onto ships from barges were over.

The schooner *Mary H. Diebold* was one of the last sailing ships to put in at the phosphate dock, circa 1920. *Courtesy of Boca Grande Historical Society.*

Bradley had other plans for Gasparilla Island. Early on, he recognized the potential of snow-white Boca Grande beaches, historian Robert Fischer wrote in a January 2006 *Pirate Coast Magazine* story.

In 1907, Bradley incorporated the Boca Grande Land Company to develop home and business sites for railroad and terminal employees. Second Street homes—now Banyan Street—were built for railroad executives.

Although the island was undeveloped, Boca Grande township had been surveyed and platted in 1897 by civil engineer and future Florida governor Albert Gilchrist.

As the railroad neared completion, Bradley built a small hotel at Palm Avenue and Fourth Street to accommodate officials and prospective land buyers. Bradley's Hotel Boca Grande opened in 1911, and its immediate success encouraged Bradley to follow through on his visions for a resort.

Bradley dreamed of building a luxurious hotel in keeping with his cousin Henry Bradley Plant's Tampa Bay Hotel constructed in 1891. Plant's grand hotel, with its distinctive Moorish minarets, is now the University of Tampa.

In 1912, Bradley opened the Gasparilla Inn at Fifth Street and Palm Avenue, while the Hotel Boca Grande was renamed the Little Inn and became an annex for the more stately inn.

By the 1920s, upper-crust Bostonians like the Crowninshields and their Delaware du Pont cousins, the Sharps, bought beachfront tracts on which they built castles in the sand.

Fisher families left the village of Gasparilla on the north end for new Lee and Tarpon Avenue homes on fifty-foot-wide lots. Better to be close to the action downtown. The rich would need the help.

Bradley wasn't the only entrepreneur who saw dollar signs. On Christmas 1926, Captain William Clement Sprott, the marshal of Mulberry who daily dealt with gunfights in his central Florida phosphate mining town, made a career move to Boca Grande and with his wife, Anna, opened the Sprott Hotel on Palm Avenue to cater to vacationers and recreational fishermen.

The Sprotts also built the Palmetto Inn at the southwest corner of Fourth and Palm Avenue and bought the Quick Hotel across the street, renaming it Hotel Palm. The house next door became the first office of the *Boca Beacon*.

In 1979, when I was a fledgling student journalist at the University of Florida, I helped *Boca Beacon* founder Marnie Banks put out the first issue. Banks had ink in her blood. The late and beloved Marnie was the niece of Pulitzer Prize–winning editorial writer and *St. Petersburg Times* editor Gene Patterson, who also served as managing editor for the *Washington Post*. Patterson was responsible for the continued printing of the Pentagon Papers in the *Post* just as President Richard Nixon blocked the *New York Times* from publishing them.

Like Bradley, Captain Sprott was a visionary who recognized another island need and filled it. Sprott owned the Ford automobile dealership in Bartow and decided Boca Grande needed cars, even though a bridge wouldn't be built for another thirty years.

In January 1930, Sprott established the Boca Grande Ferry Company Inc. with a landing at Loomis Cut near Thirty-Fifth Street. The mainland dock was in Placida, near old Gasparilla Fishery.

Sprott started with a one-car barge he towed behind his yacht *Beth*. One way, five dollars; round trip, eight dollars. He expanded to a two-car barge, then a sixty-four-foot, nine-car ferry named *Catherine*.

Sprott added a second ferry, the *Saugerties*, in 1947, previously in operation on the Hudson River between Saugerties and Tivoli, New York. Along with Eugene and Captain Carey Johnson, Sprott ran the *Catherine* and the *Saugerties* until 1955, when the family sold their operation to the Florida Bridge Company.

Florida Bridge suspended ferry operations on July 4, 1958, and opened the Samuel Schuckman Causeway, allowing people to drive from Placida to Boca Grande for seventy-five cents per car and ten cents per passenger.

A bridge to the island coincided with Seaboard Airline Railway Company abandoning passenger service. The last passenger train left the island in 1958 with my two brothers, Mark and Danny, and myself, accompanied by our grandma Nellie and a basket of fried chicken, coleslaw and cornbread. Last stop: Murdock in north Port Charlotte.

After phosphate trains stopped running in the late 1970s, the railroad bed became weed-choked and useless, but it didn't go to waste. Gasparilla Inn owner Bayard Sharp handed over land south of First Street to Seaboard Coast Line in exchange for the railroad bed. He then turned the strip into a six-and-a-half-mile-long bicycle path.

No more bells and whistles from a locomotive, only the hum of wheels on a bike path meandering through mangroves lined with expensive waterfront homes and palm trees, the silence interrupted by shrieking ospreys diving for dinner.

Island historian Fischer talked with Sprott's granddaughter Jane Brouwer McVickar about the Sprott influence. "Looking back he now seems bigger than life, perhaps because of what he did for a living ultimately made him a player on history's stage," Brouwer told Fischer. "He and my grandmother came to Boca Grande when the town was very young. She founded a business on hospitality and he on getting people safely on and off the island."

But it was Italian immigrant Joe Spadaro who would rattle island bluebloods. Spadaro made a fortune building New York City sewers and paving Brooklyn roads. He was also responsible for constructing the dike on the southern rim of Lake Okeechobee.

In the early 1920s, Spadaro decided it was time to enjoy the fruits of his labor. He was familiar with the island's reputation as a playground for the rich, but his first trip to Boca Grande left a sour taste.

Karl P. Abbott served as Gasparilla Inn general manager from 1912 to 1927. In his 1950 book *Open for the Season*, Abbott described his tenure at the "little hotel on an island off the Florida coast that catered only to 'the right people.'"

Italian immigrant Spadaro failed to pass muster. When he showed up at the Gasparilla Inn front desk in clamdigger pants, he was asked to leave. According to my cousin Freddy Futch, one of America's wealthiest men shrugged and said, "Well, that's alright. I'll build a hotel of my own."

Spadaro came up with a plan to one-up the Gasparilla Inn by buying land south of First Street and building a magnificent three-story brick hotel in the shape of an *X*. It's the same land Bayard Sharp acquired and later traded for the railroad bed.

Spadaro's opulent Boca Grande Hotel lobby featured an octagonal atrium with tall palms in the center reaching for light coming through a glass cupola four stories up. Potted palms were spread throughout the ornate lobby.

The red-brick Boca Grande Hotel opened in 1930, welcoming all comers. No one was turned away. Considered the safest place to be during the 1944 hurricane, the entire island hunkered down there to ride it out.

At the start of the Great Depression, Spadaro charged four dollars a night for a luxurious room, complete with indoor plumbing. The price stayed that way until January 20, the start of winter social season, when the price jumped to six dollars.

All the "right people" showed up, and Spadaro was giddy about his hotel's success.

When Spadaro died in 1952, Boca Grande Causeway builders Robert Baynard and Samuel Schuckman bought the place and ran it until Gasparilla Inn owner Bayard Sharp took over the abandoned, run-down hotel.

In 1973, Sharp sent in a wrecking crew to raze the competition. But Spadaro had the last laugh. A crane equipped with a wrecking ball proved useless. A builder of sewers and dikes, Spadaro knew how to erect something that lasts. He had reinforced the building's brick façade with train rails and concrete.

The crane operator couldn't finish the job, so Sharp enlisted Boca Grande Fire Department volunteers, who burned it to the ground.

So much for the competition.

A few years later, Seaboard Coast Line railway pulled up stakes and their tracks. With no more railroad, the phosphate dock was dismantled. After that, central Florida phosphate was sent to the Port of Tampa or Manatee County.

With the demise of the port's phosphate operation, Boca Grande flowered into something completely different. Developers aimed their sights on Gasparilla Island.

Sunset Realty sold its holdings at the north end to the builders of the Ocean Reef Club in Key Largo. The new owner built the Boca Grande Club, which includes hundreds of units on the beach, a clubhouse with a pool, tennis courts and a marina at the site of the long-gone Gasparilla

Albatross bar in better days, circa 1920s. At the top of the picture, Cayo Costa still looks the same. *Courtesy of the Johnson family and Boca Grande Historical Society.*

village. CSX built 313 homes on the old Boca Grande Hotel property and named it Boca Bay.

Wealthy visitors bought up seventy-five-year-old shotgun homes and renovated them to their liking. Island fisher families who settled Boca Grande a century before were eased off, because they couldn't afford the property taxes that skyrocketed with home values. Even on Whitewash Alley—fisher families' name for Tarpon Avenue—a fisherman could afford a $200-a-month mortgage but not $10,000 in annual property taxes.

By the mid-1990s, the *New York Times* travel section had touted the island for its off-the-beaten-path charm. Another invasion was on the way. The 1 percent don't flinch at paying $1 million for a Whitewash Alley fisherman's shack and spending an equal amount renovating.

The neighborhood would never be the same.

MOMMA SHIRLEY'S HOECAKE

Hoecake is a large biscuit for a hungry crowd. It was a staple for those sixty workers who showed up at the port in 1905 to build the railroad. My mother, Shirley Cassady Futch, used to make hoecake when my Clearwater High School football teammates and I needed a stick-to-your-ribs breakfast.

The term *hoecake* is thought to have originated with slaves working cotton and cornfields in the South, because it was quick to prepare. Flour and water were mixed into a ball and flattened so it would fit on a gardening hoe and held over an open fire. Like that, instant bread.

But Rod Cofield says differently. In his paper "How the Hoe Cake (Most Likely) Got Its Name," Cofield writes that *hoe* was a term for a griddle and dates to 1600s England, where cakes were baked on wood or iron "hoes."

Here's how Momma Shirley did it. She would fry up a bunch of bacon in a large iron skillet and set the bacon aside. Then she'd pour out some of the grease and use the rest for frying the hoecake. Sometimes, she poured out all the grease and substituted butter.

Instead of just water and flour, mom took a couple of liberties. She would knead two cups of flour, one-third cup of water, add a little milk and a couple of eggs and form it into one thick, fat pancake. She'd turn up the heat and carefully lay the massive pancake in the hot bacon grease for fifteen or twenty seconds, then turn the temperature down to simmer. She'd cook it for a little while before flipping it over. Make sure you lift the hoecake with two spatulas every now and then to make sure you're not burning the bottom. When the bottom is golden brown, it's time to flip and cook for a few more minutes. After it's done, momma would slather the hoecake with butter and serve it with cane syrup and a plate of bacon for a breakfast that sticks.

13

WATERING HOLES

Animals of every stripe share watering holes. Gasparilla Island watering holes are no different.

Nightlife cruised along at a steady hum in the 1970s and '80s for those making the rounds from the Pink Elephant on Boca Grande Bayou to the Temptation downtown and finally the Laff-a-Lott (now South Beach) at Port Boca Grande. The extinct Albatross bar at the foot of the phosphate dock held a special place in island lore.

For eighty years, the Kozy Kitchen across from the train depot cooked homestyle breakfast, lunch and dinner and served beer. On weekends, country-western bands from Arcadia sent dancers swinging while bat-wing saloon doors flapped at a furious pace with the comings and goings of mullet fishermen and millionaires.

But the old Pink Elephant Restaurant and Bar was ground zero for the best seafood in Florida and a lounge with no limits.

In 1949, Delmar Fugate opened the Pink Elephant Bar and a few years later added the restaurant, with entrées like shrimp sauté and broiled pompano amandine.

Every day at 8:00 a.m., head bartender Forrest Stover or Delmar opened the wide-as-an-elephant's-rump screen door to the bar. Tarpon fishermen would pile in for Bloody Mary cocktails after returning from a 4:00 a.m. trip, each drink increasing the size of their fish until it was comparable to Jonah's whale.

Scott Johnson wonders if the Kozy Kitchen will be open for breakfast. *Courtesy of Janet (Italiano) Gillespie.*

Built by Delmar Fugate, the old Pink Elephant Restaurant and Bar opened in 1949, welcoming all comers, from mullet netters to billionaires, as well as presidents, including George H.W. Bush and George W. Bush. *Courtesy of Wickman Photography and Betsy Fugate Joiner.*

For more than twenty years, Stover whipped up concoctions at the Pink then passed on his knowledge to Pat Owens, Billy Kamensky, my brother Mark and myself. Stover showed us how to make Bloodys for fishermen and Manhattans for the moneyed set.

But the Pink wasn't the only show in town. Jack Harper's Millers Marina sponsored big-money tarpon tournaments. Gambling on fish was an integral part of the fun in Millers during Friday-night Calcuttas.

Today, the name is Eagle Grille and Miller's Dockside restaurants. New owners correctly add an apostrophe to the original spelling of Millers Marina.

Whidden's Marina and dance hall was a stone's throw south of Millers. "Ladies free, gentlemen 50 cents. Air conditioning and Sears-Roebuck for your comfort," the circa 1940s sign above the bait tank still reads.

Last stops: The Temptation, the Laff-a-Lott and the Albatross.

OLD PINK ELEPHANT RESTAURANT AND BAR

Islanders called Delmar Fugate's proposed Buccaneer Bar a white elephant. Too far from town. Fugate's Folly.

Fishing guides docked across the street at Bayou Avenue and Fifth Street thought Fugate had a great idea. Mostly because there would be a bar across the street.

Fugate built the Buccaneer anyway then painted it pink and renamed it the Pink Elephant after traveling to the Bahamas and Bermuda, where the bright colors of buildings inspired the name change.

D.O. to his friends, Delmar opened the Pink as a bar only, until Captain Billy Wheeler trundled over from the guide dock to cook his grouper chowder on the patio. With a nod to Wheeler's spark, D.O. enclosed the downstairs patio, installed Spanish tiles and a kitchen and opened the restaurant in 1954, said Delmar's daughter Betsy Fugate Joiner.

Fishermen loved D.O., because he treated them fairly, paying them cash for Turtle Bay oysters. Every afternoon, fishmonger Tommy Parkinson delivered pompano netted that morning. To gather a bushel basket of stone crab claws, Delmar drove his Mercury station wagon four blocks to Whidden's Marina and the Red Gill Fish House, where Captain Sam Whidden raised them in pens.

One thing remained a constant: Dining at the Pink was a fresh-as-fresh-seafood-can-be experience. Steak and prime rib were available, but why bother?

Three-quarters of a century later, the Pink is still standing, though only in name. Bayard Sharp bought the Pink in 1978 and put up a cedar-and-brass façade. A pretty palace with excellent food, just not the same.

Prior to the makeover, access to the bar meant a long walk up a concrete-and-coquina-shell walkway to another flight of stairs that led to an extra-wide screen door two people could walk through shoulder-to-shoulder.

Air-conditioning turned up to arctic provided cool relief, especially when Hunter fans whirred loud enough for takeoff. If Stover the bartender knew you, your drink was on the bar before you sat down.

The old Pink's fifty-seat dining room was on the first floor and partially underground for customer comfort. For patrons sitting at a table next to one of the jalousie windows with the topsoil outside at shoulder level, the room was cool as a cave.

After two years of renovation to relocate the dining room upstairs and move the bar to ground level, Sharp opened the new Pink in 1980.

Like that, the Pink mystique was gone, and with it the turquoise-and-pink neon sign out front that sported an elephant wearing a party hat and raising a martini glass in its trunk.

My aunt Doris Wheeler used to issue orders as manager/bouncer of the old Pink's dining room, her acidic tongue as caustic as a sailor's. Round as a bowling bowl, Doris stood five-foot-nothing. She was afraid of no man—not even her fishing guide husband, Billy.

On one occasion, Doris gave the heave-ho to Johnny Carson's *Tonight Show* sidekick Ed McMahon, who popped in on a busy Saturday without reservations and insisted on being seated. "We have no room. Go upstairs and have a drink. I'll call you."

"Don't you know who I am? I want to sit down now," McMahon demanded.

Doris boomed: "I know who you are and I still don't have any room for you. Now get the hell out of here and don't come back."

If Doris didn't like the cut of your jib, she'd probably still feed you, as long as you minded your manners and followed Pink rules. No. 1: Don't smoke in the tiny dining room.

If you lit up, Doris could be the troll under the bridge.

One chief executive officer made the mistake of continuing to puff on his cigar after Doris told him to "put that thing out. You're bothering people."

When she walked away, the CEO lit up. Doris turned, ripped the Bances Presidente from his mouth and drowned his expensive stogie in his expensive drink. "I told you to put it out. Do that again and I'll put it where the sun don't shine."

The executive shot back, "That was a $20 cigar!" to wit Doris replied, "That's right. It *was* a $20 cigar." The man was stunned. Then he broke into a smile, his guests roaring with laughter. The wrath of Doris was a badge of honor.

While the little general oversaw customer comfort and tongue-lashing, Chef Hoke "Hokey" Harrison was in charge of the Pink kitchen. His wife, Ernestine, was the host, while Betsy Joiner, my aunt Edith Silcox and her daughters Becky and Jackie waited tables and kept Doris as calm as they could.

Hoke had another talent sought out by the rich. He was a scratch golfer, which meant the wealthiest members of the Gasparilla Inn Golf Club wanted to team up with him, including longtime playing partner Alfred Vanderbilt, who insisted the clubhouse manager put Hoke's locker next to his.

After a long day on the water or links, the Pink bar was the island rendezvous. "The Pink Elephant became the gathering spot on Boca Grande," Captain Freddy Futch said in an April 2003 interview. "Guides would send their customers there for a drink, and as soon as they put away their bait and tackle, they'd be upstairs with them."

Growing up, Betsy Joiner would climb one of seven rosy-pink, leather-topped stools at her daddy's bar every afternoon for a Shirley Temple mocktail made of ginger ale and maraschino juice with the obligatory skewer of cherries. "When the bar was open, my father was always in the middle of telling a story that ended in an uproar of laughter. Then he'd start another. Growing up, I couldn't wait to have my first Moscow Mule [ice, vodka, ginger beer and lime in a copper cup].

"There was no place like the old Pink. We had so much fun. I remember Sid Catlett and Doris Wheeler jitterbugging, Billy Wheeler, too. And New Year's Eve at the Pink was special with all the locals dressed to kill."

Hovering over Stover's right shoulder behind the bar was a painting called *Pilikia*. The unsigned oil-on-plywood explained a lot about why people came to Gasparilla Island and still do.

The artist who painted it remains a mystery. Betsy Joiner saved it when the old Pink was torn down and hung it in her Whitewash Alley home.

Pilikia shows two cartoonish, red-faced men fishing on water that looks a lot like Boca Grande Pass. They have a problem. They're both hooked into the same crazy-looking creature that's on the surface and torpedoing toward them. The deck of their boat is filled to the gunwales with a crazy catch of yellow fish with red circles and black polka dots, green ones

Inside the old Pink Elephant Bar in the mid-1950s. Longtime bartender Forrest Stover (*center*) served up drinks and smiles for almost thirty years at the Pink. Captain Charlie Wheeler (*left*) of the guide boat *Quo Vadis* whoops it up with friends and tarpon charter party. *Courtesy Betsy Fugate Joiner.*

with lime-green splotches, a blue one with a sword-like snout and a large octopus lazing on the cabin.

The name on the stern, *Pilikia*, means "trouble" in Portuguese.

One character looks over at his buddy and says in the subscript, "What the hell are we drinking, anyway?"

Fishing and drinking seemed to be a common island theme. Ensuing trouble depended on the intensity of both.

A picture window near *Pilikia* held row after row of liquid courage in a rainbow of liqueurs and cordials.

An antique one-hundred-pound brass cash register was anchored in place next to the bottle prism, its glass-enclosed top revealing dollars-and-cents signs that popped up when drinks were served and the keys played. Beers: fifty cents. Mixed drinks: one dollar.

Delmar's collection of ceramic pink elephants donated by friends held court underneath a mahi-mahi mount big enough to be considered a bull. A television set was suspended on the wall next to the dorado. Taped to the bottom was a sign that read, "DRINK."

Pilikia means "trouble" in Portuguese, and these two anglers have found it. *Pilikia* hung behind the old Pink Elephant bar for decades, and every time barflies looked at it, they understood what they were in for on Gasparilla Island. *Photo by Rick Montgomery of Island TV from the original owned by Betsy Joiner.*

A pecky cypress phone booth with a glass window provided cheap entertainment as patrons tried to figure out what the heck the person inside was talking about. Dozens of phone numbers were written or carved into the booth's nicotine-stained planks.

By arriving early Saturday night, lucky patrons could cozy into a raised, rose-colored booth attached to the south end of the bar. The booth sat three—four, if you liked one another.

The jukebox was behind the booth on a rose-and-cream-colored linoleum dance floor that turned red-hot as the night wore on. The Wurlitzer dispensed two plays for a quarter that might start with Red Foley's "Salty Dog Rag" or "Milk Bucket Boogie." How about a little "Lipstick on My Collar" by Connie Francis? Hank Williams could woo with "Hey, Good Lookin'" and rue with "Your Cheatin' Heart." But Patsy Cline broke them with "Crazy."

A large wood-and-glass case hung on the south wall with all manner of stuffed fish found in Charlotte Harbor, including barracuda, permit, pompano, grouper, red snapper, squirrelfish and redfish. The bathroom doors on either side of the case welcomed "buoys" and "gulls."

A tarpon mount seemed to jump off the wall over the entrance to an enclosed patio with large round tables.

Silver kings may be royalty on Boca Grande, but the supreme ruler of the Pass was suspended above the bar on heavy chains: a twelve-foot tiger shark. When the old Pink was demolished, Millers Marina owner Jack Harper bought the man-eater and hung it over his bait tanks.

As 2:00 a.m. dropped, with revelers swinging in furious fashion, I'd scream, "Last call!"

Captain Leroy "Brownie" Brown, who lived at Whidden's Marina on a crude wooden houseboat, was a frequent guest. As he walked in, Pat Owens cried out, "Brownie. Would you like anything to drink?"

Brownie responded, "Yessir, captain. I'll drink anything."

HOMER ADDISON'S TEMPTATION GRILLE AND COCKTAIL LOUNGE

Homer Addison brought two things essential to island survival: whiskey and water.

Whiskey was the easy part. Water took an act of Congress and plenty of paperwork.

Addison and Johann Fust Community Library caretaker Tommy Cost are credited with applying for a Farmers Home Administration loan that paid for construction of a water pipe from the mainland. No longer would anyone have to depend on cisterns.

Water didn't endear Addison to islanders as much as his Temptation Grille and Cocktail Lounge. Except for a few renovations, the Temp looks the same as it did when Addison opened it in 1945.

Temptation owner Homer Addison helped bring whiskey and water to the island. "I had juke boxes and a piano and people dancing in there every night 'til two or three in the morning." *Courtesy Homer Addison family.*

That's what makes the place so attractive to anyone enjoying spicy fried shrimp and grouper.

The neon sign hanging over the bar entrance features a martini glass with a glowing olive, a beacon luring the thirsty.

Moviemakers used the sign in the opening of *Out of Time* with Denzel Washington. A camera zeroes in on the Temp's sign, then pulls back to reveal a sleepy Park Avenue late at night. It's a scene-setter for a small-town Florida murder.

With the old Pink vibe gone, the Temp became a favorite watering hole of fishing guides.

A montage of photographs on the Fishermen Wall of Fame is to the left of the bar's entrance.

Uncle Sug Futch is there, Lucky Strike cigarette in hand, the bill of his white baseball cap tilted upward. So is Phalo Padilla, a Have-a-Tampa cigar jutting from his mouth. Everyone's adopted favorite son, Captain John "Tater" Spinks, is there, too. And it seems like bait fisherman and raconteur Sid Catlett is ready to jump out of his picture and tell a story.

Guide and netter Phalo Padilla on the Temptation Bar Fishing Wall of Fame. *Courtesy the Padilla family and the Temptation.*

The Temp's a classic, complete with brass foot rail salvaged from a New Orleans drinking establishment by Catlett's right-hand man, Scott Johnson.

George "Snake" Smolzer recalled seeing plenty in his thirty-four years tending the Temp bar. He enjoyed the repartee, working customers brave enough to take a bite of whatever apple he was dishing out.

Armed with a razor-sharp wit and thin as a reptile, Snake moved like a sidewinder, his horn-rim glasses magnifying victims before he directed insults. Everyone was fair game. And if Snake had the night off, his partner-in-life and Temp bartender Paula Johnson was capable of picking up the slack and hurling her own jokes and barbs.

Most people who suffered a Snake bite didn't mind, because, officially, it made you an islander.

"The Temp was fun, because everybody knew everybody," Snake said in 2020. "The whole town was in the bar almost every day. They got the joke. And if you're around long enough, you'll get the joke, too. When I retired in 2016, it had been decades of pure joy. Just like a jail sentence."

The Temp's dining-room walls depict island life as seen through the eyes of Addison's friend Deo Weymouth. Her maiden name was Dulcinea Ophelia Payne du Pont. But she preferred "Deo" to the name she shared with Don Quixote's mythical fair lady.

One morning, Deo showed up at the Temp holding paint, palette and brushes. She was there to brighten up Addison's avocado-green restaurant. Deo knew Addison needed more business, so she painted the walls depicting her wealthy friends golfing, sunning and shelling on the beach, arriving at the train station and tarpon fishing in the Pass. There's a wonderful sketch of the Japanese Bridge over the bayou.

Deo told her friends what she had done, and they'd have to go have dinner at the Temp to see for themselves. From then on, the Temp became a regular stop for beachfronters.

Island artist Patti Middleton honored Deo's work by freshening up the characters in 1986. Middleton saved the mural a second time in 2004 after Hurricane Charley blew the roof off and rain bleached the mural.

In 1960, Addison sold the Temp to Frank and Marty Smith, who were living at South Seas Plantation on Captiva Island. They thought Captiva was overrun with tourists, which made it difficult for the naturalists to follow their daily swimming ritual.

On their first trip, they were sold on the island, because they could swim in the buff. No one on Boca Grande cared. Swimming nude had been common practice long before the Smiths bought in. Louise Crowninshield would take family and guests to Little Gasparilla Island to swim in the nude for their health.

For thirty years, Frank was behind the bar while Marty worked the door.

After the Smiths came on board, the Temp's reputation for fine seafood rivaled the old Pink's, but in a much different way.

In an effort to stand out, they took on Chef Jean Montgomery and her maître d' husband, John, who brought New Orleans–style cooking. No one could resist Chef Jean's hot crabmeat Temptation, blackened redfish, fried shrimp and grouper and goldbrick ice cream for dessert.

In 1990, the Smiths sold to Jim and Karen Grace, who knew it was best to leave things as they are. People like the familiar. "I never felt like we owned the Temptation. More like we were caretakers," Karen said in 2019. "The Temp has a living spirit. People who come over and over again understand."

The Graces sold in 2014 to Andy Duncan, son of longtime islanders Gene and Jean Duncan. Andy teamed up with new partners, Chef Kevin Stockdale and former manager Jeff Simmons, who started as a busboy in high school helping the Temp's waiters du jour, Dennis Guppy and Jimbo Wyman.

From the start, Simmons was wise enough to understand that buying the Temp meant embracing the past. "I haven't changed a thing," Simmons said in April 2019. "I'm just the custodian. The Temp belongs to the island."

Simmons said Chef Stockdale likes adding his own touch, like potato-chip-encrusted flounder or seared tuna tataki, but the all-time favorites like spicy fried shrimp and grouper have never left the menu.

"It's old-school Florida," Simmons says, "and I'm not going to let it disappear."

THE LAFF-A-LOTT (NOW SOUTH BEACH)

Bud and Mona Amen's Laff-a-Lott saloon at the south end emerged as the late-night place to be when the old Pink closed.

The Pink's transformation was a stroke of luck for the Amens. For the next twenty years, the Laff's terrazzo became the island's dance floor.

Longtime Boca Grande postmaster Bud Amen, his wife, Mona, and son Andrew made things happen at the Laff. Day and night, they served burgers, hot dogs and seafood baskets.

After the dinner crowd left, the Amens moved the tables back and served music to a sweaty, appreciative crowd.

The Amens made the Boca Bande the regular entertainment. Lead singer Mike Weddle, guitarist Ron Tierney and bassist Jennifer Tierney rocked the night away for a typical crowd of one hundred, many more on holiday weekends. When the band struck up "Jump" by Van Halen, the Laff vibrated.

Bud Amen's mother, Irene, built and named the nondescript, concrete-block Laff-a-Lott. Its initial success came on the heels of the Albatross bar's demise.

The Albatross occupied the front part of a squat, one-story clapboard building at the foot of the phosphate dock. Sailors from around the world had a place to drink while freighters waited days for holds to fill. Port workers, fishermen and beachfronters liked going there to drink and tussle with sailors.

THE ALBATROSS

A wrecking ball made quick work of the Albatross bar in 1962 while CIA operatives were training on a nearby island for the failed Bay of Pigs invasion.

Bumps Johnson owned the Albatross with its stunning view of Charlotte Harbor. But that's as far as the stunning went.

The Albatross served only beer. It didn't matter. The Port Boca Grande bar was a beautiful bird for sailors on shore leave.

It took several days to unload phosphate from train cars onto a three-foot-wide rubber conveyor belt that moved the yellow-gray mineral to six-hundred-foot ships at the end of the one-thousand-foot-long dock jutting into Charlotte Harbor.

Sailors looking for a good time didn't have far to go. "The Albatross was the first thing the sailors saw when they got off the ships," Captain Dumplin' Wheeler said in 2019. "It was at the head of dock, and as soon as they stepped onto dry ground, that's where they'd go to spend their money."

The wood building with old man Willis' general store in the rear featured all the conveniences, including an outhouse.

"There was always a fight at the Albatross," said Wheeler, who grew up on nearby Belcher Road. "One time, I had been there awhile and needed to go to the bathroom bad. I ran to the outhouse at the other end of the building, and there's this guy leaning up against the door and I can't get by him 'cause he's blocking it. I thought he was drunk and passed out.

"I had to go bad, and when I went to move him, he slid down the door. Somebody had stuck him with a knife."

Ah. The good old days.

Old Pink Elephant Shrimp Sauté

Before sailing into the sunset in 2000, Delmar Fugate left behind the recipe for the Pink's signature shrimp sauté, with shrimp playing a supporting role.

"This recipe is a combination of ideas from a number of people," Delmar said. "I put in a lot more garlic and white wine than most. I use a lot of wine."

Start with a half-pound of raw, peeled shrimp per person.

Sauce for six:

On low heat, melt 3 sticks (¾ pound) of salted butter in a large saucepan. After the butter is liquefied, add 5 cloves of minced garlic. Stir in 1 teaspoon of light brown sugar. Add ⅓ of a 5-ounce bottle of Lea & Perrins Worcestershire sauce. Add juice from 1 key lime—a Persian lime will do in a pinch. Stir ingredients until they meld. Turn up the heat until the sauce is bubbling. Add shrimp and turn heat to high. In 30 to 45 seconds, pour in at least 1 cup of white wine. Turn the shrimp over and cook for less than 1 minute. Serve in bowls with plenty of sauce, toast points on the side for sopping.

Old Pink Bloody Mary

It's imperative to make it in this order: Fill a tumbler with ice, salt top of ice, cover ice with Lee & Perrins Worcestershire sauce, juice from ½ of a key lime, vodka and Sacramento tomato juice. Shake vigorously and pour into a tall glass. Slip in a small wedge of key lime.

14

FUTCH FACTS

If a member of my fishing family was talking, Futch Facts were at the heart of a story, and laughter followed.

My brother Mark defined a Futch Fact as "a story that's accurate, but not necessarily true."

Early Charlotte Harbor fishermen were masters at inventing world-class whoppers. Storytelling was a source of pride, whether tarpon fishing in Boca Grande Pass or pulling on nets in Charlotte Harbor back bays and creeks.

If there's fish to catch, there's lying to be done. And if there's not a laugh in a lie, what's the point?

Island fishermen always ended their tall tales of adventure by looking you straight in the eye and finishing with, "Don'tcha see?"

Uncle John Alderman was the camp cook for my great-granddaddy Frank Futch's thirty-man stop-net operation.

Alderman chimed in one evening that he was familiar with New York City and the Statue of Liberty in particular. Everyone knew Alderman had never been farther north than Tampa in his life. Nevertheless, he continued on about his trip to the Big Apple.

"I jus' wanna tell ya. I lived in the flame of Miss Liberty herself. Yessir, I had my bed and my stove and I baked cathead biscuits all day long for the people who'd climb to the top. The mayor of New York was so happy he didn't charge me one dime to stay there. Don'tcha see?"

Captain Phalo Padilla (*right*) with root beer king Charles E. Hires after landing this monster kingfish. *Courtesy of the Padilla family and Boca Grande Historical Society.*

That's when Will Craig shot back, "I got one better 'an 'at." My grandfather Dan was in fish camp the night Craig told the following distortion of reality to the crew.

> *I was a logger in Oregon, and we had clear-cut redwoods growing thick on the sides of two mountains that faced each other. It took us all day and we got 'er done except for one monster tree next to where I was standin', and she's a 400-footer. Might have been 500.*
>
> *I yells down the mountain to everyone in the valley below to get the hell outa the way. I'm taking care of this one myself.*
>
> *So I start choppin' on that monster with my axe. In a couple hours, I yells out, "Timmmmm-berrrrrr."*
>
> *Well, this redwood as thick as the Empire State Building hits the ground and starts rollin' and gatherin' speed.*
>
> *It's got such a head of steam that it rolls into the valley and up the side of the other mountain across the way from me. You gotta remember, we'd clear-cut so there's nuthin' in its way.*
>
> *So it starts rolling back down that mountain and up the side of the one where I'm standin' and stops at the toes of my boots.*
>
> *Then it rolls the other way, down into that valley and up 'til it reaches near the top of that other mountain.*
>
> *Then she rolls back down and up again where I was. This goes on for three days and when that redwood finally come to a rest on the valley floor, it was no bigger around than a No. 2 pencil. Don'tcha see?*

From 1880 until it was outlawed in 1960, Florida commercial fishermen used "stop" nets to catch mullet, a fish with a gizzard that qualifies it as a bird. Maybe that's why they jump out of the water so much.

Stop-netting was backbreaking work. Hand-lining cotton and linen nets during the December mullet run meant working those nets for days at a time while living on crudely built houseboats called "lighters."

The men would fish day and night from small skiffs, returning to a makeshift, engineless lighter to eat, sleep and tell stories, their only form of entertainment.

By anchoring a lighter in Turtle and Bull Bays, the netters stayed close to their work.

Will Craig offered up another one he swore happened. He went on and on about whaling in the Mariana Trench, the deepest part of the Pacific Ocean.

Craig said the first whale he ever struck with a harpoon sounded thirty thousand feet. "When I finally pulled up Moby Dick's brother by myself, the pressure must have been so great at the bottom that the whale surfaced flat as a pancake. Don'tcha see?"

In the 1950s and '60s, Dick Cooper found his calling as cook in Willie Salter's fish camp. One time, Cooper said he invented the jet engine and that the president of the United States awarded him a medal. When everyone asked him how the engine worked, he said, "I don't really know."

Another time, Cooper struck up a conversation with legendary liar Albert Padgett.

> *Albert. I jus' wanna tell ya one thing. I got caught in the 1929 hurricane that nearly wiped out the Gulf Coast.*
>
> *When that hurricane topped out at near 200 mph, it stripped all the leaves off the mangroves in the Ten Thousand Islands.*
>
> *Me and Totch Brown got blowed into them mangroves and while we's hangin' on for dear life, all our clothes was torn off and we was left wearing nuthin' but our birthday suits.*
>
> *But that's OK 'cause the grouper and snapper was blowed into them mangroves, too, and got impaled on the branches. We just climbed through and picked 'em like they's apples. Don'tcha see?*

Padgett shot back, "That ain't nuttin' to brag about. I was in Kansas once when this cyclone blowed up and stays in one spot for a week. When it finally petered out, there was a hole deep enough to drop in a skyscraper. So we climbed down trying to find China, but we never did. How 'bout 'at?"

That's how Padgett always ended his stories. He preferred "How 'bout 'at?" to "Don'tcha see?" Don'tcha see?

Padgett told my cousin Dumplin' about the time he was crossing Boca Grande Pass in a howlin' nor'wester and sunk. Padgett's stout vessel, *Dinky*, was fifteen feet long and little more than planks powered by a five-horsepower Briggs & Stratton lawnmower engine that Padgett started by pulling on a rope. *Dinky* had a two-blade propeller that pushed it along at a steady two knots.

> *According to Dumplin's recounting, Padgett said he caught 5,000 pounds of sheepshead off Cayo Costa before dark. He was crossing Boca Grande Pass in heavy winds, lightning and rain. Now five thousand pounds of sheepshead was a stretch, because Dinky was so small and leaked so bad, she couldn't have held more than fifty pounds. Anyway, Padgett told me he's*

in front of the phosphate dock when the propeller came off and where it's forty feet deep. I asked him, "What'd you do?"

Padgett told me, "I dove overboard, found it, put her back on and went to the fish house. Made more money than I ever had before." Albert would tell one lie and back it up with another.

Mark Futch's favorite story about Padgett is "every bit the truth because I saw it with my own eyes." Padgett lived in a shack on the shore of Bull Bay and didn't have two nickels to rub together, but he had a $10 million view.

Padgett threw this party and he started with a big bonfire on the beach next to his wood lean-to attached to a dock where some of the planks were even nailed down.

So Padgett and the other hermits who lived on Cape Haze would drink moonshine and get good and drunk. Then someone would pluck a fiddle, and pretty soon these fishermen were dancing with one another. The only question centered around who's turn it was to wear the blue gingham dress Padgett bought for such occasions.

There are two Futch Facts that absolutely are true.

The Futches measure time and distance differently than most people.

In the 1950s, U.S. 41 was called the Tamiami Trail, or just the Trail, a two-lane road meandering between Tampa and Miami.

So Freddy Futch asked his Uncle Dan Futch how long it took to drive from Boca Grande to Tampa.

Dan replied, "If someone's with you, one case of Budweiser."

There's another one about Aunt Clara Futch catching her husband, Dunk, red-handed sitting on the beach with a young woman who was sunbathing in front of the inn beach club.

Consider this: Dunk fished about 350 days a year, and his skin was as dark as the ace of spades.

About the time Dunk plopped down next to the woman half his age, Aunt Clara wandered down to the beach looking for Dunk, who hadn't shown for breakfast.

Standing on the seawall with arms crossed, Aunt Clara looked down at Dunk, who had his back turned, and she said in a calm voice, "Dunk. Whatcha doin' down there?"

Without missing a beat, Dunk turned and replied, "Workin' on my suntan." Don'tcha see?

Cathead Biscuits

In southern parlance, dinner is lunch and supper is dinner. Either way, a table is never complete without biscuits.

Cathead biscuits that Uncle John Alderman cooked while he was "living in the flame of Miss Liberty herself" are made with the same ingredients as hoecake, except catheads are baked while hoecake is fried.

2 cups flour
2 tablespoons shortening or lard
1 cup buttermilk or milk
Pinch of salt

Mix, then throw flour on a cutting board and knead. Form into cathead-sized biscuits and bake 15–20 minutes at 400 degrees.

15

SPLIT PERSONALITY, BEACONS AND THOSE DAM STREETS

Two Florida counties claim Gasparilla Island, a split that began two hundred years ago when Andrew Jackson was Florida's military governor. Lines of demarcation are all around Boca Grande. Geographic, familial and philosophical differences abound. It runs with the insular territory.

Perhaps the most mystifying boundary is the geographical line slicing through seven-mile-long Gasparilla at Grouper Hole, landing the island into Lee and Charlotte Counties. Anything south of the southernmost Boca Grande Club property line is in Lee County. The club and everything to the north is in Charlotte County.

Gasparilla Island's first line in the sand was drawn ten years after the United States acquired Florida from Spain in 1819. General Andrew Jackson had savaged the Seminoles during the First Seminole War in 1817–18 while looking for and seizing runaway Black slaves living with the Seminoles. First, he had to beat back Spanish forces from Pensacola to near St. Augustine. With hard-charging Jackson on their trail and without the necessary forces to defend their territory, the Spanish gave Florida away for a song.

In 1819, Secretary of State John Quincy Adams signed the Florida Purchase Treaty with Spain in return for $5 million in claims by U.S. citizens against Spain.

In 1821, Florida became a U.S. territory and a survey was undertaken. Surveyors ignored one detail. The survey took only the Florida mainland into account and failed to mention the barrier islands skirting the Gulf

Coast. Almost a decade later, the federal government decided to divide Florida into smaller pieces.

In 1829, the U.S. government determined that the Key West Customs District covered too much territory. It included thousands of square miles of sea and coastline from the Dry Tortugas seventy miles west of Key West to St. Marks Lighthouse south of Tallahassee in Florida's Big Bend. The feds wanted to divide the vast expanse of the Key West District in half, because it was too big for one administrator to oversee.

Jackson had already been appointed military governor of Florida two years prior to the United States acquiring Florida, and his administration was on board with a federal decision to change Florida's internal boundaries. This in turn led to cutting the island into unequal parts, a 70–30 separation, with 70 percent in Lee County.

Surveyors were dispatched. After an extensive, walking inspection through dense pine forests, estuaries and mangrove islands in 1829, they took their findings to mapmakers, who drew a series of dashes that cut through Charlotte Harbor.

Everything to the north of those dashes would be in the St. Marks Customs District; everything to the south was part of the Key West Customs District.

But the surveyor made no mention of the sandbars and barrier islands jutting into the Gulf a mile or so west of the mainland. None of the islands from Marco Island near Naples to Anclote Key north of Clearwater Beach were included in the 1829 map. After the line of demarcation separating Key West from St. Mark's became official, someone thought it might be a good idea to see what was along the Gulf Coast.

When a new survey was conducted, inspectors decided there was no reason to trudge across dense Charlotte Harbor mangroves to conduct another full-fledged look at the coastline. They simply gave the mapmaker the same information previously gathered in the 1821 survey. That mapmaker then drew arbitrary dashes that made an angular jog and cut across the north end of Gasparilla Island at present-day Boca Grande Club, as evidenced in antiquarian maps at the Vernon and Edna Jane Peeples Collection at the Punta Gorda History Center.

One of those arbitrary dashes was drawn through the north end of Gasparilla and was the keystone to the island's division.

Former Florida legislator and my cousin Vernon Peeples was a Charlotte Harbor historian and collector of early Florida maps. At the Punta Gorda History Center, you can spend an entire day looking over the Peeples Collection, which includes two hundred maps and charts of Florida dating from 1683. Peeples died in 2015 at age eighty-five, leaving his treasure trove to the people of Florida.

The Punta Gorda native's knowledge of boundaries was unparalleled, the go-to guy with regard to how Florida was sliced up.

"In order to make the Gasparilla Island survey fit with the mainland survey, the surveyor drew a slash [across Gasparilla Island at the north end] so the lines would come together," Peeples said in March 2007 for *Pirate Coast Magazine*. "But the survey was inaccurate. Charlotte Harbor was remote, and people didn't pay much attention to geopolitical boundaries. It wasn't until the railroad was built to the island in 1907 that Lee County officials discovered the south part of the island was in Lee County and they wanted a piece of the action."

There's more to the story. Unlike the 1829 map, an 1855 Florida map in the Peeples Collection shows several barrier islands at the mouth of Charlotte Harbor. An 1855 sketch shows the progress of the Florida survey, and charts in NOAA's Historical Map & Chart Collection also confirm the existence of Gulf barrier islands.

Florida lawmakers had decided in 1855 that two massive counties—Manatee and Hillsborough—needed to be subdivided. They were too big, stretching eighty miles from Fort Myers to Tampa Bay. Legislators used the original 1829 line of demarcation separating the two customs districts, which is today the same line separating the island into two counties. So one-third of the island was in the St. Marks District to the north and two-thirds of the island in the Key West District to the south. But the island remained in Florida's largest county, Manatee.

That is, until 1887, when the legislature broke up Manatee, Hillsborough and DeSoto Counties into several counties. They named one of them Charlotte, which was in the St. Marks District. The southern part of Gasparilla Island that had been in the Key West Customs District was named Lee County after Robert E. Lee, commander of the Confederate States Army and the Army of Northern Virginia.

But that's a story of a different kind of separation.

BOCA'S BEACONS

Port Boca Grande Lighthouse lit the way for mariners starting in 1890. Eighty years later, the beacon was falling into the water and island kids went there to get lit.

In the summer of 1989, over wine and cheese, Boca Beacon founder Marnie Banks told staffers Daniel Godwin and Marilyn Hoeckel of her dream to turn the lighthouse into a museum. It was the birth of the Barrier Islands Park Society—BIPS to almost every islander. Saved by the society during a three-year renovation in the 1980s, it still sends its signal to mariners.

On the other hand, the tall rear range light south of First Street is a castoff from Delaware that went up in 1927 after a long boat ride to Miami then Gasparilla Island.

Since 2008, Sharon McKenzie has been keeper of the Port Boca Grande Lighthouse Museum and executive director of BIPS, charged with keeping the lamp burning. There are plans to shore up the place even more and shift the museum's focus.

For McKenzie, island history tells us a lot about us as humans. "I'm a firm believer that to know where you're going, you've got to know where you've been," McKenzie said. "It's a beautiful thing to hear stories from our past. Telling stories was the only form of entertainment for so many early islanders, especially the fishermen.

"There were such characters on this island from all walks of life, rich and poor, all of them unique and wonderful storytellers. Today, we get so caught up in technology and the rat race, trying to get ahead, trying to be good capitalists, that we forget these stories. The lighthouse museum is here to keep island history alive."

THOSE DAM STREETS

Blame it on "Red" Hall. He's the Dam guy.

There are a lot of stories about how the Dam Streets got their name. The one that seems to hold the most water centers on Laurence "Red" Hall building his home along one of the recently-dug canals south of First Street. Lee County had already named the three new thoroughfares along the canals Second, Third and Fourth Streets Southeast, but no one knew that, even new property owners.

The unpaved shell road in the middle had a stake at the entrance that read "Number 3."

When a delivery driver from Robbins Lumber was looking for Hall's address, he stopped at the Barnichol hardware store and asked for the street where "Red" Hall was building a home because he had a load of wood for him. Hall's fishing guide, Captain Ted Bylaska, happened to be in the Barnichol and overheard the man.

Port Boca Grande Lighthouse Museum shows the way home during a June 2021 sunset. Author's collection.

"Damfino," Bylaska told the driver, then explained how to get there by taking a right after going over the railroad tracks at First Street.

"But what's the name of the street?" the driver asked Bylaska, who responded with, "I told you. Damfino. It's the second road."

As it happens, Red Hall, Dr. Hank Wright and Dr. I.M. Essrig were waiting for the delivery from Tampa when the truck driver showed up. He told them the story, and the three men laughed and thought it was a good name. Damfino Street stuck.

When word got out at a cocktail party that Hall wanted to name his street Damfino, Kay Reed, who lived on Fourth Street Southeast, said, "Who cares?" The last street turned into Damficare. Those on Second Street Southeast who had been protesting the name changes finally caved, and it became Damfiwill Street.

Like so many things on Gasparilla Island, no one really gives a damn what you do. Island life is all about keeping yourself in good company and taking long siestas in the nap capital of the world. Don'tcha see?

ABOUT THE AUTHOR

David Futch is a fourth-generation Gasparilla Islander. After graduating from the University of Florida, Futch covered government and politics in Florida, Alaska and California. He lives in Santa Monica, California, with his adored wife, Sally Stewart.